LAYOUT:making it fit

ROCKPORT

GLOUCESTER MASSACHUSETTS

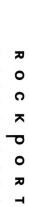

ROCKPORT PUBLISHERS

LAYOUT:making it fit

FINDING THE RIGHT BALANCE BETWEEN CONTENT AND SPACE

Carolyn Knight
Jessica Glaser

Copyright © 2003 by Rockport Publishers, Inc.

First paperback edition printed 2005.

First published in the United States of America by
Rockport Publishers, Inc., a member of
Quayside Publishing Group
33 Commercial Street
Gloucester, Massachusetts 01930-5089
Telephone: (978) 282-9590
Fax: (978) 283-2742
www.rockpub.com

Library of Congress Cataloging-in-Publication Data available

ISBN 1-59253-185-7

10 9 8 7 6 5 4 3 2 1

Design: **Bright Pink**

Cover design: **Jerrod Janakus**

Cover images: **Why Not Associates**
John Brown Citrus

PRINTED IN CHINA

There are many people and organizations that have helped us during the writing of this book, and we would like to take this opportunity and space to thank them for their support, enthusiasm, and contribution. We have appreciated all the assistance and encouragement from Rockport Publishers, the University of Wolverhampton, our families, and the designers listed below, who so willingly submitted work (whether we were able to include it or not).

344 DESIGN • AIGA, BOSTON CHAPTER • APPETITE ENGINEERS • BAUMANN & BAUMANN • BBC DESIGN BRISTOL • BECK GRAPHIC DESIGN • BELYEA • BLACKCOFFEE • ADAMS OUTDOOR ADVERTISING • BRUKETA & ZINIC DESIGN MANUFACTURE • BURGEFF CO. • BÜRO FÜR GESTALTUNG • CARLOS SEGURA • CPD DESIGN • CROATIA AIRLINES • DDSN INTERACTIVE • DENNIS ICHIYAMA • DIGITAL VISION • DISINFOTAINMENT • DWELL • ELEMENTS LLC • EXQUISITE CORPORATION • FELTON COMMUNICATION • FISHTEN • FITZGERALD-HARRIS DESIGN • FUTUREBRAND • GEE + CHUNG • GREENFIELD/BELSER • GROUP BARONET • GUMPTION DESIGN • HAT-TRICK DESIGN • HAYMARKET PUBLISHING • HÉPA! DESIGN • HOLLER • HORNALL ANDERSON DESIGN WORK • HUME LAKE CHRISTIAN CAMPS • IDAHO • IDENTIKAL • INFOGRAPHICS DESIGN • INPRAXIS, RAUM FÜR GESTALTUNG • INTERBRAND • I[E] DESIGN • JERRY TAKIGAWA DESIGN • JOAO MACHADO DESIGN, LDA • JOHN BROWN CITRUS PUBLISHING • KARACTERS DESIGN GROUP • KATIE GARDNER DESIGN • KROG KRAKOVSKI • KYM ABRAMS DESIGN • LAUREY ROBIN BENNETT DESIGN • LIFT COMMUNICATIONS • LOVE • LOWERCASE INCORPORATED • MATT AND GEORGE • MEDIA CELL, LTD. • MEDIA CO., LTD. • METALLI LINDBERG • MIKE SALISBURY, LLC • MIRKO ILIC CORP. • MONSTER DESIGN • MOTOKO HADA • NIKLAUS TROXLER DESIGN • ODED EZER DESIGN STUDIO • OFFICE OF TED FABELLA • ORANGE SEED DESIGN • ORIGIN DESIGN • P22 • PALAZZOLO DESIGN STUDIO • PAPRIKA • PARHAM SANTANA • PETER KING AND COMPANY • PHILIP FASS • PILAR MUNOZ • PING PONG DESIGN • PISCATELLO DESIGN CENTRE • POCKNELL STUDIO, LTD. • PURDUE UNIVERSITY • RECHORD • RED BEE STUDIO • RED COMMUNICATIONS • RIORDEN DESIGN GROUP, INC. • RIPTIDE COMMUNICATIONS • ROUNDEL • SAGMEISTER, INC. • SAYLES GRAPHIC DESIGN • SCANDINAVIAN DESIGN GROUP • SCORSONE/DRUEDING • SILVIA VALLIM DESIGN • SK VISUAL • SPLASH INTERACTIVE • STOLTZE DESIGN • STUDIO INTERNATIONAL • STUDIO VERTEX • TEIKNA DESIGN, INC. • THARP DID IT • THE INDEPENDENT NEWSPAPER • TRICKETT AND WEBB • TRUDE COLE-ZIELANSKI • TULLETT DESIGN • UNIVERSITY OF WASHINGTON SCHOOL OF ART • WAGNER DESIGN • WHY NOT ASSOCIATES • WILSON HARVEY • WORKWRITE • XTRCT DESIGN • Y+R 2.1 • Z3 • ZGRAPHICS, LTD.

contents

IT HAPPENS AT THE SAME TIME EACH YEAR—**carrier bags of press cuttings, handwritten notes in turquoise ink on the back of envelopes, the odd floppy disk, and many, many emails arrive in our office, all demanding attention. Doesn't March come round quickly? Please don't misunderstand us; we are delighted to receive all these bits and pieces, as we really enjoy working with the enthusiastic client who dispatches them. But there is no doubt that the information to be included in the *WCSP Annual Review* will take both of us some effort to decipher!**

We can be certain of one thing—there will be a lot to say in the resulting report, with some sections needing to contain great amounts of information while others that are no less important saying considerably less. This is the project that during the past few years has caused us to stop and analyze one element of design in particular—the use of space. The final design will include pages that are packed with text and images, as well as some that have only a few lines of information and one or two images.

INTRODUCTION

On reflection, we realize this is a very common situation. On almost a daily basis, we face the prospect of dealing with little information within a generous space and lots of information in a comparatively limited space. Looking at other design work, we can also see this is obviously not unique to us, and that tackling these issues often forces the production of strong design, encompassing the brave and unexpected. Space is a crucial element within every layout, as integral as typeface selection and the treatment of images, but it seems that when there is either an excess or a shortage of it, designers can become particularly resourceful and imaginative. Our intention in this book is to highlight many different examples of work at both ends of the spatial scale and to try to examine some of the thinking and methodologies involved in producing these pieces.

DESIGN FIRM **WHY NOT ASSOCIATES**
● DESIGN **WHY NOT ASSOCIATES** ●
CLIENT **MALCOLM McLAREN** ●
PROJECT NAME **MALCOLM McLAREN**
POSTER

With many projects, we may curse the fact that we have either too much or too little space for our own design aesthetic and ambition, but often we impose our own spatial restrictions. When dividing information, we will certainly go out of our way to avoid even distribution, actively engineering "space rich" and "space poor" layouts. This use of composition can significantly influence the visual message. Tone of voice, target market, and appeal can all be modified by spatial factors to create a wide spectrum of impressions such as exclusive, luxurious, expensive, lively, popular, cheap, reliable, or caring. Gunther Kress and Theo Van Leeuwen, in their book *Reading Images: The Grammar of Visual Design*, refer to the significance of these design decisions.

"VISUAL STRUCTURES REALIZE MEANINGS AS LINGUISTIC STRUCTURES DO. . . FOR INSTANCE, WHAT IS EXPRESSED IN LANGUAGE THROUGH THE CHOICE BETWEEN DIFFERENT WORD CLASSES AND SEMANTIC STRUCTURES IS, IN VISUAL COMMUNICATION, EXPRESSED THROUGH THE CHOICE BETWEEN, FOR INSTANCE, DIFFERENT USES OF COLOR OR DIFFERENT COMPOSITIONAL STRUCTURES."

Whether imposed or chosen, the use of space can wield a lot of power in communicating intended messages. In the Why Not Associates poster celebrating the work of Malcolm McLaren, we can see that the comparatively full composition with a number of layers and interactions of text and image generates a lively and spirited impact. Some of the practices of punk and the design techniques that McLaren used when working with Vivienne Westwood have been used as the basis for this poster to capture the mood of the time. This is a nonconformist message, presenting relevant information mixed with the irrelevant in a partially accidental way. As a consequence, the space also has a paradoxical quality—on one level it can be perceived as controlled by the designer, but on another it seems like an effect of serendipity.

"FOR THIS POSTER, WE DESIGNED A TYPE TREATMENT THAT WAS THEN PRINTED OVER ANY RUNNING SHEETS THAT WERE FOUND LYING AROUND AT THE PRINTERS," says David Ellis of Why Not Associates. "THE POSTERS WERE PRINTED OVER ALL KINDS OF THINGS, FROM SOMBER REPORT AND ACCOUNTS PAGES TO COMBINATIONS OF NAPPY [DIAPER] AND FOOD PACKAGING. THE RESULTING POSITIVE AND NEGATIVE SPACES THAT INEVITABLY OCCUR IN VARIED PLACES ON DIFFERENT POSTERS HAVE A GREAT DEAL TO DO WITH THE CHARACTER OF THESE DESIGNS." Ellis concludes, "WE KNEW THE RESULTS WOULD BE CHAOTIC AND CONFUSING, SO WE JUST KEPT THE TYPE BOLD, CLOSED OUR EYES, AND THOUGHT OF ENGLAND!"

Conversely, if we focus on the cover and one of the introductory sections of an Icebreaker Clothing catalog, it is apparent that the extravagant use of space is markedly responsible for lifting the perception of the products into a "must have" category. The generous space suggests quality and style. Through its intelligent composition, the space carefully controls the viewers' awareness of sensitive art direction, photography, cropping, printing, use of paper, and layout. Even the wide letter and line spacing conveys a sense of precision and deliberation that reflects on the product and tells the reader that nothing is left to chance in the manufacture of these garments—every detail is covered.

"OUR FIRST OBJECTIVE WAS TO TELL THE ICEBREAKER STORY IN A POWERFUL MANNER. CLARITY AND NO UNNECESSARY DESIGN DETAIL WAS OF UTMOST IMPORTANCE," says Rachael Paine of Origin Design, New Zealand. Although all the design elements work together, the generous use of space predominates; on the right page, the cut-out figures, the crisp minimal typography, and the red bar are dynamically presented in a large matte silver space. On the left page, as on the cover, all over photographs depict comparatively small figures in vast environments, with the great spaces that nature creates echoing the sentiments of power, wonder, and individuality.

As we reviewed work that illustrates creative use of space, one unexpected and interesting discussion point arose more than once. In which section should a submission be placed? Much of the work that we have included easily fits into both "The Designer's Dream" (excessive space) and "The Designer's Dread?" (shortage of space) sections of the book. The contrasts of scale, texture, and spatial distribution that created complementary paces and rhythms to make "reading" more interesting were the very scenarios that created our dilemma. As a consequence, some of our submissions have a presence in both sections of the book—albeit showing differing elements, of course.

DESIGN FIRM **ORIGIN DESIGN** ● DESIGN **ROBERT ACHTEN** ● COPY **ICEBREAKER** ● CLIENT **ICEBREAKER** ● PROJECT NAME **ICEBREAKER CATALOGUE**

As for the project that we mentioned at the beginning
of this introduction—the annual review that over the
past few years has made us particularly aware of the
use space in design—we have decided that it cannot
escape making an appearance (see page 131). After
all, it has to take responsibility for a great deal!

In the first section of this book, we have collected examples that skillfully handle the challenge of working with small amounts of information in extravagant spaces. In each case, the criterion for selection has been that the basic requirement of the brief is to convey a comparatively short message, leaving plenty of scope for constructive use of space and embellishments. Very often, designers may choose to augment content with more words or images to elaborate or enrich, but providing that the fundamental point is brief, they are still included in this section.

promoting. The treatment of the content includes the choice of typefaces, weight, scale, color, composition, style of mark making, materials, processes, and more, that can be changed and adjusted endlessly to amend the connotations. Even minimal manipulations can have significant impact on the visual language. A 10 percent change of tone or a point-size reduction can take an element into a different level hierarchically and dramatically affect its accessibility to the viewer.

Recognizing and appreciating consequences of fine-tuning within the design process can be difficult to put into words. The linguistic analogy of the sentence (syntagm) with its possible alternatives for each word (paradigmatic alternatives) is helpful in understanding the ramifications of minute, intricate changes. For example, using "Simple Simon walks a dog" as the syntagm, merely replacing the preposition "a" within the paradigm to "the" significantly alters the meaning. This is no longer just any dog, but a specific dog. In exactly the same way, when a designer changes just one element or treatment—a line to a dot, blue to

DESIGN FIRM **HAT-TRICK** ● DESIGN **GARETH HOWAT, DAVID KIMPTON, JIM SUTHERLAND** ● COPY **D&AD** ● CLIENT **D&AD** PROJECT NAME **XCHANGE**

THE DESIGNER'S dream

Designers often dream of having a project with plenty of space and few limitations, as the perception is that this presents greater opportunity to explore style and visual dynamics. Space that is free to be more concerned with aesthetics than function is inviting to designers, as it seems to provide further scope for innovation and imagination. Maybe there is an inherent wish to design something that is up-market, and this appears to be far more possible within generous areas of space. Whatever the initial reaction, in our experience, the process of creating successful layouts with very little given content is amazingly difficult.

It is a complex and challenging responsibility to ensure that space does not come across as being either negative or distracting and that elements are not simply included or repeated for the sake of filling space. Designers have numerous alternatives that help create successful layouts. Composition, hierarchy, contrast of scale and tone, the addition of elements, typefaces, colors, processes, and more all have a role to play. Recognizing the implications of these design choices from both objective and subjective viewpoints is key to this decision-making process.

It is helpful to consciously define two main aspects of a layout for consideration—the content and the treatment of that content. Words, all kinds of images and marks, format, and space come together under the banner of content, generally denoting the primary message of the layout—what, for example, a book is about, what a package contains, or what a Web site is

red, light to bold, or a photograph to an illustration—the semantics change. A general impression of expensive can be cheapened; an ordinary layout can become distinctive, or the clarity of a message can devolve into confusion.

Kenneth Hiebert says in *The Basel School of Design and Its Philosophy: The Armin Hofmann Years, 1946–1986,* "THE ACT OF SEARCHING FOR AN APPROPRIATE STRUCTURE FORCES THE DESIGNER TO MAKE THE MOST BASIC ENQUIRY ABOUT AN OBJECT OF MESSAGE, TO ISOLATE ITS PRIMARY ESSENCE FROM CONSIDERATION OF SURFACE STYLE. IN THIS EXHILARATING BUT ARDUOUS PROCESS, THE DESIGNER IS ENGAGED IN DEFINING MEANING AT BOTH THE SIMPLEST AND MOST UNIVERSAL LEVELS."

Spatial distribution has to be given significant consideration in all layouts, but plays a more dominant role within designs involving less information. In these designs, inevitably there are a greater number of compositional options and, consequently, many more visual meanings. It has been interesting to note that dynamic layouts featuring unusual positions can suggest innovative, forward-thinking approaches, while

more predictable central orientations can imply static, less sophisticated attitudes. All relationships are in part determined by their spatial arrangement—space occurs between letters, words, and lines, around groupings, and within images. Technological advances now enable the designer to have precise control over spatial distribution within images and text—overlapping letters or even adjusting the space within the bowl of a letterform may create a different visual message. Sensitive detailing can enhance connotations such as busyness, tranquility, efficiency, and fun.

DESIGN FIRM **EXQUISITE CORPORATION** ● DESIGN **RILEY JOHN-DONNELL** ● COPY **JEREMY LIN** ● CLIENT *SURFACE* MAGAZINE ● PROJECT NAME *SURFACE*

A number of the submissions included in this section use processes very powerfully. If a letter or a shape is cut out instead of printed, or has a contrasting surface to the material on which it is produced, it seems to become far more significant. The 2002 D&AD Exchange brochure demonstrates this very well; it is as if the letter *X* takes on several roles. It is seen as the letter of the alphabet, the shape that has a number of connotations, a cut-out hole, and, most interestingly of all, a shaping of the space around it and a framing of the many views through it. Distinctive cut-out and folded pieces control space in a fascinating and interactive manner. Very often, minimal use of text and imagery can produce enjoyable coherence and cohesion.

The D&AD Xchange brochure had to capture the interest of a professional design audience. A fine balance was required between the serious, informative content and an intriguing but not distracting treatment. The cover uses yellow space to lead to the cut-out *X*, which in turn, by its very nature, takes the viewer through all the pages in a fascinating manner. Inside, each double page makes generous use of white space with the same cut-out *X* acting as the initial letter to relevant titles. At least two-thirds of the space is, in effect, empty, but the intrigue of the cut-out *X*, the large scale of the title, and the contrasting detailing come together to ensure comfortable viewing of this piece.

Another treatment of content worth noting has to do with the organization of elements and the use of systems. From the outset, the very first mark that begins a layout creates both character and a set of relationships. All subsequent design decisions are then made in response to those initial parameters. This does not mean that a layout becomes static and dull, but simply that every element has a "sense of belonging." If we look at the lively moving card designed by Katie Gardner, we see that every mark has a reason for adopting its size, color, and position. Sometimes the inherent qualities within given letters or images inspire certain links, like the section of the number *2* that becomes the stem of the arrow and dictates the perpetuation of its angle. In other instances, distances between items, as well as from the edge of the frame, are replicated. Alignment points, weights, colors, tones, and scales all have been selected in relation to each other in order to achieve the most satisfying cohesion.

Small amounts of information that are accommodated within plenty of space might be as a result of choice or of being imposed. When designers have the luxury of selecting a format, they will inevitably have a view of the intended message and how it is going to be communicated. Problems often arise when a section within a predefined format suddenly has to contain very little and yet still retain value and relevance within the overall scheme. One of the most challenging aspects of design occurs when a project has to accommodate information-heavy sections, as well as those that are information light. However disparate the essence of these sections may be, it is essential that they look as if they belong to "the same set." The same levels of information, styles, groupings, and design systems need to be applied in a varied yet consistent manner. The cover of a brochure or magazine can frequently be an example of this; despite generally having to include little text or image, it should provide a "taster" of the design content and at least some of the treatments that will be seen on the inside pages.

The covers of *Surface* magazine make interesting and effective use of contrasting textures, using mixes of varnishes applied to octagonal and circular patterns and areas that reflect shapely compositions to come. Upon initial exploration of the interior, it becomes obvious that in addition to regular cohesive styling, distinct references are made to this theme. Pages have images within octagonal shapes, cutouts such as chairs that capture sections of octagons, and a number of linear elements that form a whole or part of these shapes predominate.

The cover of *Surface* issue 25 predominantly uses earth tones and depicts a model wearing a shirt patterned with concentric octagons. These shapes are then repeated using a mix of transparent, matte, and gloss varnishes. Having to impart a minimal amount of information, it is still vital that the cover "belongs to" the rest of the publication. The designer has made careful choices of color, pattern, composition, and cropping to establish a range of visual cues that can be developed throughout the magazine.

It has been fascinating to receive so many fresh and invigorating examples of the use of extravagant space from around the world. We recognize a universal spatial understanding that transcends individual

DESIGN FIRM **KATIE GARDNER DESIGN** ● DESIGN **KATIE GARDNER** ● CLIENT **PERSONAL PROMOTION** ● PROJECT NAME **PERSONAL MOVING CARD**

cultures. So do designers, wherever they live, have the same dreams? Do they yearn for very little given content that may give them more opportunity for self-expression? When reading the submission comments, we have been comforted to discover that even if this is true, reality generally proves to be far more challenging than anticipated!

DESIGN FIRM **PAPRIKA** ● DESIGN
**LOUIS GAGNON, FRANCIS TURGEON,
FRANÇOIS LECLERC** ● COPY
ANDRE MAROIS, HOWARD SCHRIER
● PHOTOGRAPHER **MARTIN LAPORTE**
● CLIENT **YELLOW** ● PROJECT NAME
YELLOW CATALOG

Yellow, a popular chain of economy shoe stores, briefed Paprika to set a new style for their catalogs. "PREVIOUS VERSIONS WERE SEASONAL AND SHOWED A HUNDRED PRODUCTS IN THIRTY PAGES," says Joanne Lefebure, president of Paprika. "WE HAD VERY LITTLE SPACE TO WORK WITH. THIS TIME, HOWEVER, THE PROBLEM WAS REVERSED: THIRTY PAGES TO HIGHLIGHT THE BRAND AND PRESENT ONLY TWENTY PRODUCTS."

The pages were successfully filled through the generous availability of space, which enabled a synergy of dynamic changes of scale, orientation, cropping, and minimal type. Color was used both in photographs and text to anchor the products to their intended market. With both formal and leisure wear, harmonious color palettes were selected to show Yellow shoes to best advantage—each shot also embraced the use of a small amount of contrasting vibrant color. The cover cleverly contained numerous unwritten visual messages associated with market appeal. Many of these messages had been captured as a direct result of brave use of scale and cropping. It is easy to see how this brochure created "new visual territory" for Yellow.

Cultureshock was an arts and culture festival that was connected with the extremely successful Commonwealth Games 2002 in Manchester, U.K. "IT WAS IMPORTANT TO CONVEY THE VARIOUS STRANDS OF THE PROGRAM ECONOMICALLY WITH A MINIMUM MEDIA EXPENDITURE," says David Simpson of Love.

The simple message was conveyed typographically in a powerful, direct, and retro manner, using bold slab serif letterforms to generate an eye-catching interplay of color and pattern. Initially adopting large type, Love went on to use tight leading and interword spacing to "eat up" the space, using the change of color to separate themes.

Simpson notes the influence he has drawn from designers such as Saul Bass, Paul Rand, and Milton Glaser. There are also distinct parallels to design styles used within publicity material for the thriving Manchester club scene.

DESIGN FIRM **LOVE** ● DESIGN
DAVID SIMPSON ● COPY
DAVID SIMPSON ● PHOTOGRAPHER
MARTIN LAPORTE ● CLIENT
CULTURESHOCK ● PROJECT NAME
CULTURESHOCK POSTER

DESIGN FIRM **BÜRO FÜR GESTALTUNG**
● DESIGN **CHRISTOPH BURKARDT,
ALBRECHT HOTZ** ● CLIENT **AGD
ALIANZ DEUTSCHER GRAFIKER**
● PROJECT NAME *AGD ALIANZ
DEUTSCHER GRAFIKER* MAGAZINE

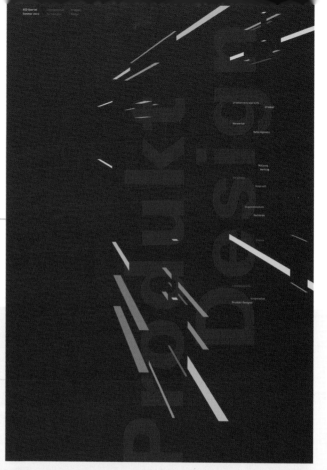

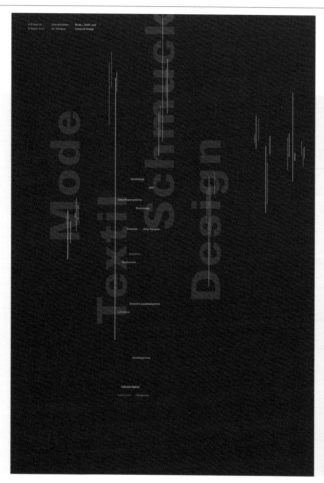

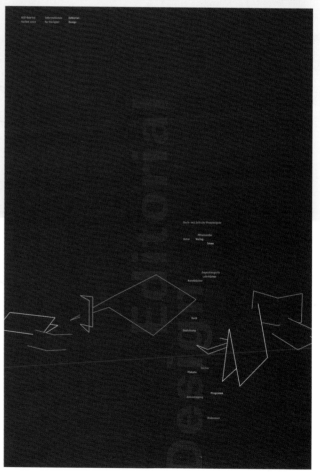

AGD **is a large-format magazine (12" × 17", 30 cm × 43 cm),** and Büro für Gestaltung chose to emphasize its scale through the use of small, accurately positioned text, minimal imagery, and very subtle areas of large type. The space created is not white space but a palette of deep, rich tones. "ALL THE ELEMENTS ARE DESIGNED WITH A LOT OF RESPECT FOR THE 'WHITE' (IN THIS CASE, VERY DARK COLORED) SPACE, WHICH CHANGES ONLY SLIGHTLY FROM ISSUE TO ISSUE," says Albrecht Hotz, a designer for Büro für Gestaltung.

Touches of vivid colors are introduced in a way that brings each quarterly issue to life. There is no doubt that the semiotics of this piece reinforce the fact that this stylish publication is aimed at a professional design audience.

corn flakes
da agricoltura biologica

250g ℮

senza
zucchero
saccarosio
aggiunto

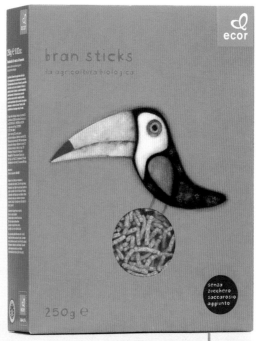

bran sticks
da agricoltura biologica

250g ℮

senza
zucchero
saccarosio
aggiunto

Cereal boxes are among the largest items to be piled into our supermarket carts, and they are generally covered in a plethora of brightly colored graphics. It is refreshing to see the available space in Metalli Lindberg's designs being used very differently, with considerable areas of flat color surrounding simple type and illustration.

"IN LINE WITH A GRAPHIC APPROACH ALREADY ESTABLISHED FOR ECOR'S OTHER FOOD PRODUCTS, THE CEREAL RANGE WAS CONCEIVED WITH THE YOUNGER CONSUMER IN MIND," says Derek Stewart, art director at Metalli Lindberg. Far from appearing as empty spaces, the flat colors complement the lively illustrations, and elements come together in a style reminiscent of children's books. It is a clever use of the "learn to read" genre, where the text is synonymous with the picture; remember the animal image and it becomes an instant reference for the content of the box.

rice crispies
da agricoltura biologica

250g ℮

senza
zucchero
saccarosio
aggiunto

anellini
di miglio
da agricoltura biologica

250g ℮

senza
zucchero
saccarosio
aggiunto

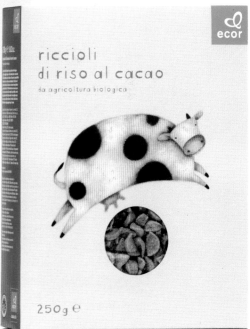

riccioli
di riso al cacao
da agricoltura biologica

250g ℮

DESIGN FIRM **METALLI LINDBERG**
● ART DIRECTOR **DEREK STEWART** ● DESIGN
FRANCESCA SPINAZZÉ ● ILLUSTRATOR **ALESSANDRA CIMATORIBUS** ● CLIENT **ECOR SPA** ● PROJECT NAME
ECOR CEREALS

As a product, water has to be one of the simplest, purest, and, "cleanest" substances on the market. Within the packaging, labeling, and advertising for Reebok Fitness Water, Karacters has successfully used generous, uncluttered space to portray these attributes. "BECAUSE WE WANTED TO SHOW AS MUCH OF THE CLEAR BOTTLE AS POSSIBLE, WE KEPT THE LABEL AREA VERY CONTAINED," says Matthew Clark. "THE PRODUCT NEEDED TO LOOK FIT AND CLEAN, WITH A FASHIONABLE EDGE THAT'S APPROPRIATE AS AN ACCESSORY IN THE GYM," he continues.

The ads are particularly striking, building solely on the metaphoric contexts of weights, trainers, and tennis balls. The composition of all three is structured and minimal, cleverly making use of icy blue tones to connote a cool, refreshing, sporty efficiency. Without a doubt, the overall simplicity and spatial effect reinforces the importance of quality and style that automatically accompanies the Reebok brand.

DESIGN FIRM **KARACTERS DESIGN GROUP** ● DESIGN **MATTHEW CLARK** ● CLIENT **CLEARLY CANADIAN BEVERAGE CORP.** ● PROJECT NAME **REEBOK FITNESS WATER**

DESIGN FIRM **NIKLAUS TROXLER DESIGN** ● DESIGN **NIKLAUS TROXLER** ● ILLUSTRATION **NIKLAUS TROXLER** ● CLIENT **KENNY WHEELER QUARTET** ● PROJECT NAME **KENNY WHEELER QUARTET**

"I WANTED TO PRODUCE KENNY WHEELER'S POSTER IN AN ILLUSTRATIVE WAY," says Niklaus Troxler, **"THAT EXPRESSED THE SOUND OF HIS MUSIC."** Clearly capturing the spontaneity of Wheeler's style of play, Troxler has chosen to adopt this expressive manner of drawing for both text and image, filling the poster with a persistent-looking overlaid line.

Despite few words being included in this focused portrait, the vitality of mark making not only fills the physical space but also provides the viewer with a real sense of the character of the music and the atmosphere of the location. The fact that Troxler has left few areas of his poster empty leads the reader to believe that Wheeler's improvisational sound will permeate every corner of the venue. Troxler adds, "THE LIGHT BLUE ON THE BLACK BACKGROUND MAKES THE POSTER 'BLUESY.' "

DESIGN FIRM **SCANDINAVIAN DESIGN GROUP** ● ART DIRECTION **MUGGIE RAMADANI, PER MADSEN** ● DESIGN **PER MADSEN, MUGGIE RAMADANI** ● CLIENT **6 AGENCY** ● PROJECT NAME **6 AGENCY PORTFOLIO**

6 Agency is a Danish photographic agency with a multidisciplinary ambition that differentiates it significantly from the mainstream. Neatly packaged boxes of photographs, evocative of cigarette packaging, are small, yet manage to establish and maintain a great sense of dramatic space throughout. The photographers' cards are held together by the strong use of flat color, with each unfolding to reveal a variety of work and crucial information. With a number of cards contained in each box, the distinctive characteristics of format and spatial generosity are multiplied, enhancing the contemporary air of this unusual piece.

DESIGN FIRM **IDENTIKAL** ● ART
DIRECTION **NICK AND ADAM HAYES** ●
COPY **ADAM SMELLMAN** ● ILLUSTRATION
IDENTIKAL ● PHOTOGRAPHY **ANTON
WANT** ● CLIENT **EMAP ACTIVE** ●
PROJECT NAME *PS2* MAGAZINE,
COLLECTOR'S EDITION

**In Nick Hayes's own words,
"WE USED BOLD TEXT
ALONGSIDE VIBRANT
PHOTOGRAPHY AND
ILLUSTRATION TO HIDE THE
FACT THAT THERE WAS LITTLE
OR NO GIVEN INFORMATION
TO BE INCLUDED."** We have
selected a couple of typical double-page
spreads from this *PS2:* Playstation2
World Launch Collector's Issue to
demonstrate how Identikal has produced
some very powerful and exciting layouts
in response to their challenge. The inside
front cover opens to an explosion of cyan,
purple, white, and black radiating out
from a PS2. Sound-wave lines, fine mesh
3-D structures, and linear representations
of appropriate hardware fascias all
illustrate the Arthur C. Clarke quote,
"ANY SUFFICIENTLY ADVANCED
TECHNOLOGY IS INDISTINGUISHABLE
FROM MAGIC." In the second spread,
unpredictable angular shapes of red and
black configure with basic text and
imagery to echo the sentiments of "Earth
Totom" — that PS2 has the technology to
take its players to other realms!
Throughout the book, bold imagery
generally supported by minimal text
cleverly elaborates on chosen themes and
provides the viewer with an experience
that attempts to mimic the PS2
experience.

"ANY SUFFICIENTLY ADVANCED TECHNOLOGY
IS INDISTINGUISHABLE FROM MAGIC"
ARTHUR C. CLARKE

PS2 HAS THE TECHNOLOGY TO TAKE ITS PLAYERS TO OTHER REALMS.
SO WHAT PLANET ARE YOU ON?

'EARTH TO TOM...'

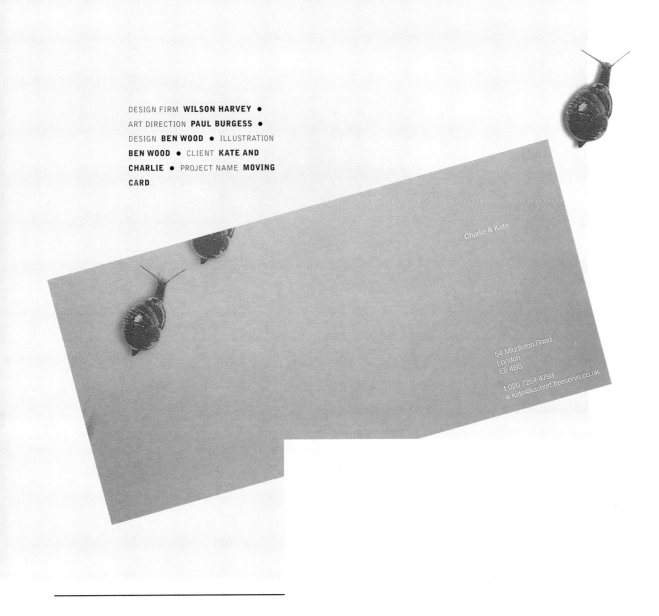

DESIGN FIRM **WILSON HARVEY** •
ART DIRECTION **PAUL BURGESS** •
DESIGN **BEN WOOD** • ILLUSTRATION
BEN WOOD • CLIENT **KATE AND**
CHARLIE • PROJECT NAME **MOVING**
CARD

Charlie & Kate

54 Middleton Road
London
E8 4BS
t 020 7254 4793
e kate@kashort.freeserve.co.uk

we've moved

By using the white side of the card for just address labeling and the smudged line,
"WE'VE MOVED," Paul Burgess and Ben Wood of Wilson Harvey are making distinctive and
practical use of the generous proportions of this space. It is not until the recipient turns the card
over that the surprising and witty message is fully apparent. Kate and Charlie are seen moving off
the edge of the card, carrying their homes on their backs! "PRIMARILY, THE MOST
CHALLENGING ASPECT WAS GETTING THE 'GAG' ACROSS IN TWO PARTS WITHOUT IT
BEING TOTALLY OBVIOUS. USING BOTH SIDES OF THE POSTCARD ALLOWED THE HUMOR
TO WORK," Burgess says with a smile.

The Estée Lauder Web pages appear lively, colorful, and busy. Jihyun Lee from Riptide tells us, "AS THE SITE WAS LACKING WRITTEN INFORMATION, WE ENHANCED THE VISUAL ATTRACTION BY USING A CONSIDERABLE AMOUNT OF IMAGES AND COLORS." In the introduction we talked about the frequent need for designers to augment given information in order to create appropriate and successful channels of communication. Riptide has done just that, embracing characteristics from current Estée Lauder advertising and promotions to support and embellish the given text. Decorative large-scale flowers are juxtaposed with product shots, models, and type headings to create a visually stimulating space.

DESIGN FIRM **RIPTIDE COMMUNICATIONS** ● ART DIRECTION **DOUGLAS LOCKYER** ● DESIGN **JIHYUN LEE** ● CLIENT **BOSTON CONSULTING GROUP** ● PROJECT NAME **ESTÉE LAUDER WEB SITE**

"THE DESIGN LANGUAGE HAD TO FIT THE THEME OF OBSESSION, AS WELL AS THE SPECIFIC TOPIC OF CHOCOLATE," says Gill Bar-Shay of this conceptual magazine for Riptide Communications. Very little hard content is being communicated in these two double-page spreads, leaving the subsequent space to be filled with type and imagery that by its very nature and configuration conveys a real sense of urgency. Paradoxically, all elements were no doubt selected and positioned with a great deal of consideration and attention to detail, but the apparent inaccuracies of angles, line spacing, sizes, focus, and spatial distribution come together to give the impression of a lack of control.

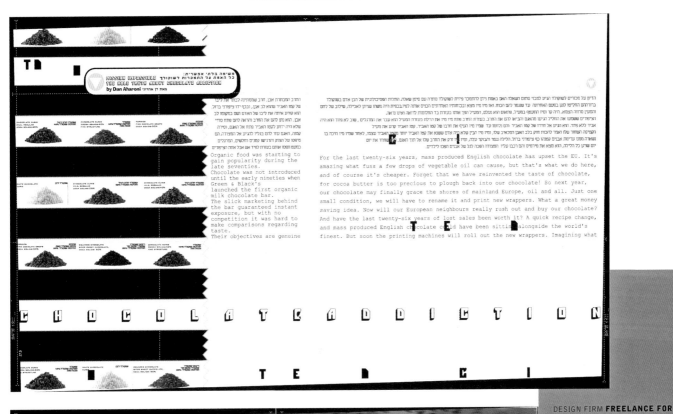

DESIGN FIRM **FREELANCE FOR RIPTIDE COMMUNICATIONS** ●
DESIGN **GILL BAR-SHAY** ● CLIENT
SELF-PROMOTION ● PROJECT NAME
OBSESSIONS **MAGAZINE: CHOCOLATE**

As this double-page spread is in black-and-white only, texture and tone are extremely significant. The composition is spacious, and the dark tones of the bird, the large letter *m*'s, the square brackets, and word "birdies" initially guide the viewer from one to the other, around the pages as a whole. The white space is integral to creating the visual journey, which cleverly leaves the reader poised to take in the main thrust of the article in the lighter, less obtrusive tones of the text. The vitality of the angled and flowing lines of type adds interest and meaning to the visual-verbal pun set up in the heading "Humming Birdies."

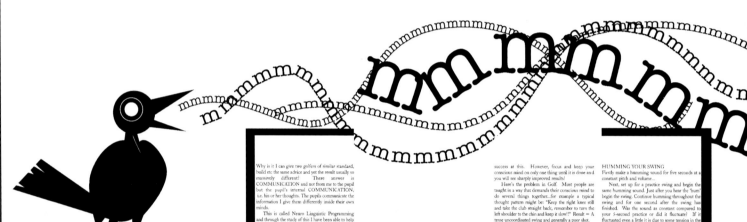

YOU WANT TO PLAY BETTER GOLF? TRY ADDING A VOCAL TO THE RHYTHM OF YOUR SWING. BY SCOT CRANFIELD
ILLUSTRATION MICKEY BOY G.

Humming
Birdies

Why is it I can give two golfers of similar standard, build etc the same advice and yet the result usually so massively different? There answer is COMMUNICATION and not from me to the pupil but the pupil's internal COMMUNICATION. i.e. his or her thoughts. The pupils communicate the information I give them differently inside their own minds.

This is called Neuro Linguistic Programming and through the study of this I have been able to help golfers not only understand the swing changes they needed to do but also how to think about them to get the best results.

There is no doubt NLP has helped me achieve better results. However, that's not the whole story, I have studied and tried to understand how other aspects of the mind are designed to work and I have developed some unbelievably simple concepts that, when applied, should work for everybody - and, yes, I really do mean everybody.

Through my articles in Bogey I want to help you lower your scores by understanding and using your mind differently. It may even improve other aspects of your life!

In this article I am going to give you the basics of how your mind works and why traditional methods don't work as well.

Many of you will be familiar with learning the terms 'conscious' and 'subconscious' mind, but it is essential to understand how they work. Let me give it to you in a simple way.
The conscious mind is for focusing your attention.
The subconscious makes things work to match your focus.
The conscious mind can only focus on one thing at a time.
The subconscious can focus on a multitude of tasks.

Through our daily lives we constantly push our conscious mind to focus on more than one thing at a time i.e. listening to someone on the phone whilst reading a letter, but we will only ever have moderate success at this. However, focus and keep your conscious mind on only one thing until it is done and you will see sharply improved results!

Here's the problem in Golf. Most people are taught in a way that demands their conscious mind to do several things together...for example a typical thought pattern might be: "Keep the right knee still and take the club straight back, remember to turn the left shoulder to the chin and keep it slow!!" Result = A tense uncoordinated swing and generally a poor shot.

The next thing you must understand is that your subconscious mind is like a servant to your conscious - it listens and carries out each thought as an order. In our example the subconscious keeps getting different messages from the conscious mind. The subconscious works best when it is left to work things out.

For example, let's look at something your subconscious mind does - walking. You consciously decide you want to go to the kitchen. Do you then consciously decide when to bend your knees, what muscles to use, when to transfer your weight - no, of course not, your subconscious mind does all the work.

So how do we apply this knowledge to help our golf? One of the hardest challenges you will first have to overcome is the control factor. Up to now may of you have been trying to swing the club and hit the ball through a matrix of conscious thoughts. To fulfil your potential you must realise you gain control (subconsciously) by giving up control (consciously).

The exercise I am going to give you to improve your golf game in this edition, when done correctly, will have you doing only one thing consciously and leaving the subconscious mind to use the appropriate muscles to swing the clubhead.

HUMMING YOUR SWING
Firstly make a humming sound for five seconds at a constant pitch and volume.

Next, set up for a practice swing and begin the same humming sound. Just after you hear the 'hum' begin the swing. Continue humming throughout the swing and for one second after the swing has finished. Was the sound as constant compared to your 5-second practice or did it fluctuate? If it fluctuated even a little it is due to some tension in the swing almost certainly caused by the conscious mind switching its focus to something else like a certain position you may have worked on even years ago.

Your task is to re-train your conscious mind to do only one thing throughout the swing and that is to produce a humming sound of constant pitch and volume. The better you get at this the more the subconscious will take over the responsibility of swinging the golf club, and I think you will find it does it far better than you can consciously.

Obviously progress onto hitting balls whilst humming audibly. Notice what part of the swing you fluctuate in and on the next shot focus especially on humming 'through' that area.

Eventually you will be able to produce a humming sound of constant pitch and volume while hitting probably some of the most enjoyable shots of your life.

Finally, so your friends don't think you are completely mad you can do this inside your head, but only after at least two 30-minute sessions where the sound is audible. Doing it inside your head is probably advisable on the course! Having said that I have coached European Tour Players who have had top-10 finishes humming out loud (gently) on every shot! Can you use it on the course? Yes. Will others think you are crazy? Possibly! Does it work? Definitely!

Until next time. Hummmmmmmmm. ➧

DESIGN FIRM **MEDIA CELL** ● DESIGN
MICKEY BOY G ● CLIENT ***BOGEY***
MAGAZINE ● PROJECT NAME ***BOGEY***,
"HUMMING BIRDIES"

DESIGN FIRM **INFOGRAPHIC DESIGN**
● ART DIRECTION **LEANNE BARNETT**
● DESIGN **LEANNE BARNETT, PETER
CAMPBELL** ● COPY **JENELLE
BECKER** ● ILLUSTRATION **PETER
CAMPBELL** ● DOCUMENTATION
PHOTOGRAPHY **HAMISH TA-MÉ** ●
CLIENT **SYDNEY OLYMPIC
BROADCASTING ORGANISATION** ●
PROJECT NAME **INTERNATIONAL
BROADCAST CENTRE, SYDNEY
OLYMPICS 2000, GRAPHIC
TREATMENTS AND WAY FINDING
PROJECTS**

**A huge architectural space certainly provides a
challenging layout!** Up to ten thousand
broadcasters and technicians operated daily from this
immense former warehouse during the Sydney Olympics,
and it was necessary for all graphics to be legible to
visitors from any country. "SIMPLICITY AND
CONTINUITY ARE CRITICAL TO THE NAVIGATION
IN THIS KIND OF LOCATION," says Peter Campbell of
Infographic Design. "INTEGRATION OF VISUAL AND
TYPOGRAPHIC STYLES, USING COLOR-CODING
AND HIERARCHICAL SYSTEMS WITHIN VAST
STRATEGICALLY POSITIONED PANELS AND
BANNERS, HELPS PROVIDE ORIENTATION AND
CONFIDENCE." The Infographic team employed
vibrant color across panels that dwarfed many spaces
and clearly defined locations when viewed from afar. At
the same time, they provided simple yet informative
signage intended to be viewed more closely.

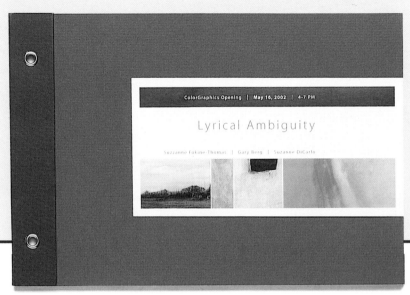

DESIGN FIRM **BELYEA** ● ART
DIRECTION **PATRICIA BELYEA** ●
DESIGN **RON LARS HANSON** ●
PHOTOGRAPHY **VARIOUS STOCK** ●
CLIENT **COLORGRAPHICS SEATTLE** ●
PROJECT NAME **COLORGRAPHICS
SEATTLE ART INVITATIONS**

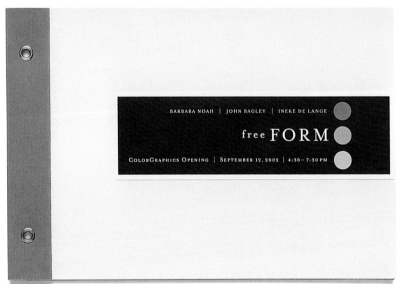

ColorGraphics is a premiere printing company that supports the arts. These three brochures double as invitations and are a very special integration of art, media, processes, and design. "THE FIRST SPREAD FOR EACH ARTIST ONLY INCLUDES THE ARTIST'S NAME AND A SINGLE PIECE OF ART. WORKING WITH MINIMAL DESIGN ELEMENTS SUCH AS GEOMETRIC FINE LINES AND RESTRAINED EXPANSES OF COLOR, STRIKING LAYOUTS ARE CREATED," enthuses Patricia Belyea. "ALTHOUGH THESE INVITATIONS CONTAIN VERY LITTLE INFORMATION, THEY ARE DESIGNED AS THEIR OWN LITTLE PIECES OF ART."

The main thrust of the little booklets is to display the works of art, yet it is just as important to set the stage and present pieces in a way that will reinforce their quality and individuality

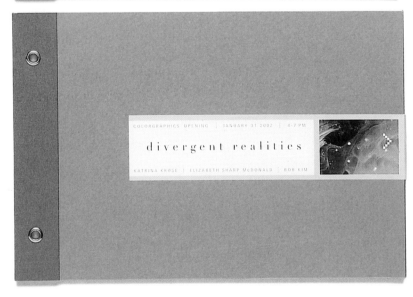

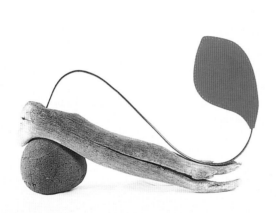

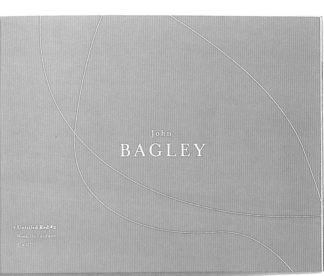

John
BAGLEY

• **Untitled Red #2**
Wood, cloth and wire
9" x 15"

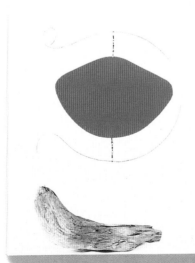

My creations come from inspirations gained
while exploring and participating in my
natural surroundings.

There are no intentions when I set forth.
I find it exciting to see what grows out of
independent elements as I bend, shape and
combine them. I like finding materials that
have been discarded or forgotten, and
bringing life and mobility to them.

Through my pieces I wish to convey
simplicity and fluidity. The beauty of life
is that everything is in a constant state of
change. Enjoy these sculptures for what they
are and for whatever they represent to you
now, because they are certain to change over
time. The metal will oxidize, the wood will
decay and the paper will fade.

Untitled Red #1
Wood, cloth and wire
12" x 3"

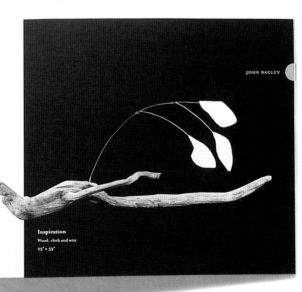

JOHN BAGLEY

Inspiration
Wood, cloth and wire
23" x 59"

DESIGN FIRM **APPETITE ENGINEERS**
● ART DIRECTION **KEIKO HAYASHI**
(SFMOMA) ● DESIGN **MARTIN**
VENEZKY ● CLIENT **SAN FRANCISCO**
MUSEUM OF MODERN ART ●
PROJECT NAME ***OPEN*** **NO. 1, "WHEN**
WILLIAM GEDNEY DIED," "ONCE
THERE WAS"

These two opening spreads to different articles in *Open* magazine are striking in their use of space and comparatively minimal information. Initially, it appears that the large orange type is responsible for the dynamics, but true to virtually all design, it is the subtle attention to detailing that brings the pages to life. Many design decisions, including letter and line spacing, are judged visually with an eye for sensitive and crucial groupings, weights, and color choices. In both instances, on the opposite pages bleed photographs are carefully positioned and cropped to complement the type.

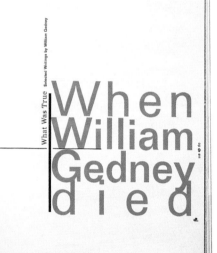

What Was True Selected Writings by William Gedney

William Gedney, SAN FRANCISCO (detail), 1966–67

When William Gedney died

A Conversation with Sol LeWitt
by Gary Garrels

From February 19 to May 21, 2000, SFMOMA visitors will have the rare opportunity to view forty years of work by Conceptual art pioneer Sol LeWitt. The long-awaited SOL LEWITT: A RETROSPECTIVE, the first comprehensive survey of LeWitt's work since 1978, presents over two hundred works—ranging from the well-known wall drawings and structures to photographs, books, and works on paper—from each phase of the artist's career.

Gary Garrels, SFMOMA Elise S. Haas Chief Curator, has been working with LeWitt for over four years to organize this ambitious exhibition. Garrels and LeWitt sat down together in September 1999 to discuss the artist's work, his creative process, and the retrospective.

DESIGN FIRM **INTERBRAND NEW YORK**
● DESIGN **KIM KELSE** ● CLIENT **SPI**
SPIRITS ● PROJECT NAME
STOLICHNAYA VODKA

With no specified copy or structure beyond the powerful brand name Stolichnaya, Interbrand was given the challenge of designing packaging that would redefine the way Americans buy Russian vodka. As Michael Lucas of Interbrand says, "WHEN YOU ARE GIVEN VERY LITTLE INFORMATION, YOU CREATE IT! AND FROM THE STOLICHNAYA NAME AND QUALITY PRODUCT CAME A BRAND THAT CREATED AND FILLED ITS OWN SPACE."

On one level, the viewer merely sees a bottle containing clear liquid with a label indicating product category, brand, and name. On another level, carefully chosen design decisions use the space in a way that creates a sense of quality and a contemporary feel. Instead of being straight, the tall, slim, clear glass bottle narrows towards the neck to create angled sides. The angle on the third character of the Russian version of the product name is reflected in the label shape, as well as in an icon created to capture the "fire in ice" mystique, and the positioning of the brand name. The layout remains simple and "spacey," maximizing the sophisticated visual semantics.

DESIGN FIRM **BBC DESIGN BRISTOL**
● DESIGN **JEAN CRAMOND** ● CLIENT
ABSOLUTELY PRODUCTIONS ●
PROJECT NAME **CREDITS FOR
TRIGGER HAPPY TV**

"WE WERE SPECIFICALLY ASKED THAT THE TITLE SEQUENCE SHOULD NOT GIVE AWAY ANYTHING ABOUT THE PROGRAM," says Jean Cramond of BBC Design Bristol, "SO THE BIGGEST CHALLENGE WAS TO FILL THIRTY SECONDS WITH CAPTIVATING GRAPHICS THAT WORKED WITH THE SOUNDTRACK."

Animated configurations of the words "Trigger Happy TV" use as much of the screen as possible, including 3-D space, as the letters zoom in and out to give the sequence depth. Simple, bold sans serif capital letters in a limited palette of red, white, and black build up to finally spell out the title, establishing a visually strong brand.

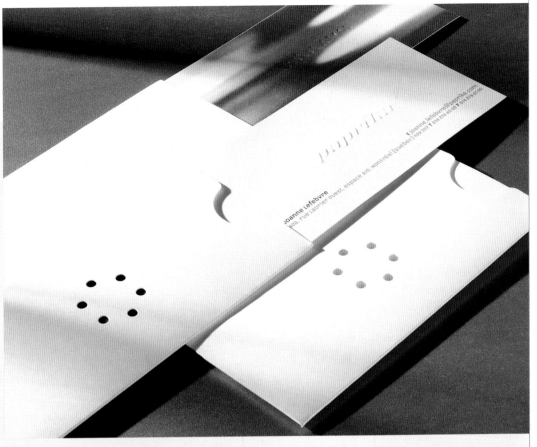

There are a number of interesting and pertinent ingredients in the application of Paprika's stationery. It is, however, the way in which these elements spatially correspond with each other across all items that really produces the visual enjoyment. Where practical, formats are horizontal and long; type runs in long lines; the envelope label stretches across three quarters of the landscape format and wraps around the end; and although not a long word, "paprika" is designed to flow with distinct emphasis on the length. All these lines then lead the viewer around the white or colored space to six-hole groupings that are literally cut through the stock, like the tops of spice jars. The concept is simple but clever, making sense of the unusual company name.

DESIGN FIRM **PAPRIKA** ● ART DIRECTION **LOUIS GAGNON** ● DESIGN **BOB BECK, ISABELLE D'ASTOUS** ● CLIENT **PAPRIKA** ● PROJECT NAME **PAPRIKA STATIONERY**

DESIGN FIRM **WHY NOT ASSOCIATES**
● COPY **MARY SHELLEY** ●
PHOTOGRAPHY **PHOTODISC, THE**
POWELL BROTHERS ● CLIENT
PLAZM MAGAZINE ● PROJECT NAME
PLAZM POSTER

Exploring an aspect of cloning technology, this double-sided poster is designed by Why Not Associates for inclusion within *Plazm* magazine. Making dramatic use of space and juxtaposed imagery in a variety of sizes, the piece includes text from the original story of Frankenstein, in the novel by Mary Shelley. In some respects, a lot of information is presented, but it is for the purpose of attracting the viewer and provoking thought on the subject, as opposed to putting over quantities of facts. Copy flows over and through images, allowing the poster to be viewed on different levels, while the generous amount of white space helps to establish the accessibility and hierarchy.

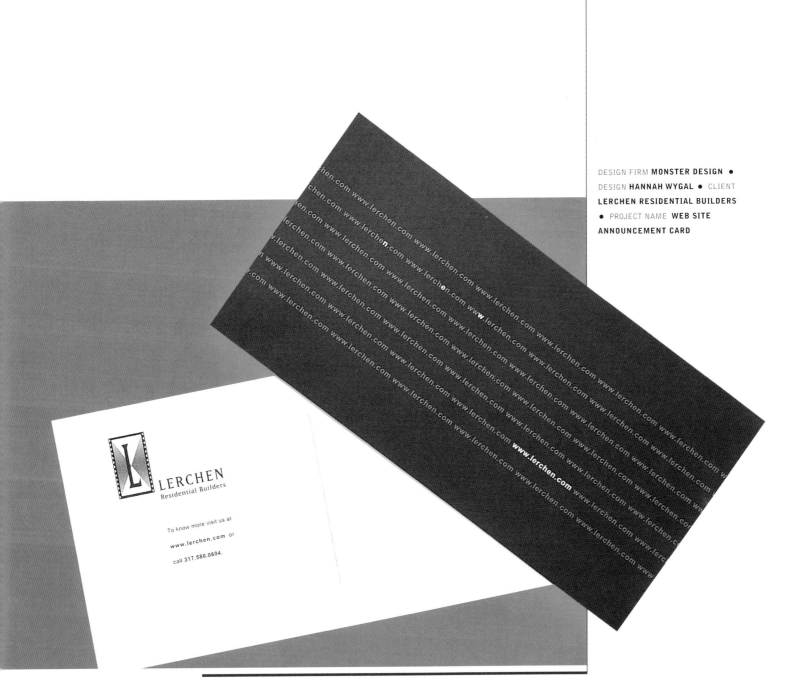

DESIGN FIRM **MONSTER DESIGN** ●
DESIGN **HANNAH WYGAL** ● CLIENT
LERCHEN RESIDENTIAL BUILDERS
● PROJECT NAME **WEB SITE**
ANNOUNCEMENT CARD

The only content that Monster Design has used on this giant postcard is Lerchen Builders' Web site address, generating a visually pleasing and compelling single-color piece. Seven widely leaded lines of small type that repeat the URL run across the center of the card. A strategically placed white URL, along with three very carefully highlighted letters—*n, e,* and *w*—are pulled out to top the visual hierarchy. Every aspect of the generous space becomes active in creating an environment that not only puts over the succinct information, but also brings it to life in a way that is memorable.

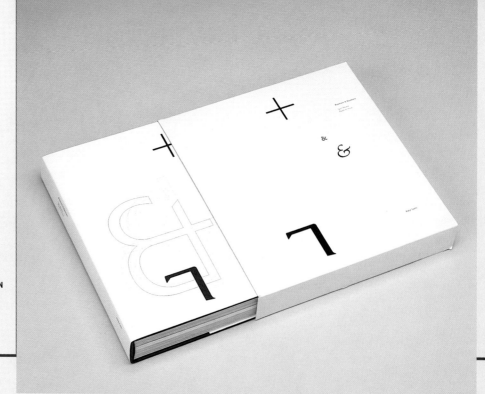

DESIGN FIRM **BAUMANN & BAUMANN**
• COPY **BAUMANN & BAUMANN** •
ILLUSTRATION **BAUMANN & BAUMANN**
• PHOTOGRAPHY **BAUMANN &**
BAUMANN • CLIENT **BAUMANN &**
BAUMANN • PROJECT NAME
SELF-PROMOTION, *ROOM TO MOVE*

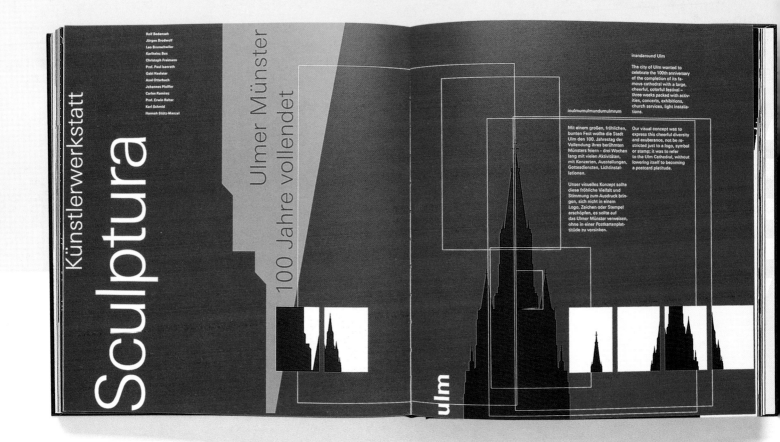

Künstlerwerkstatt

Sculptura

Rolf Bodenseh
Jörgen Brodwolf
Leo Brunschwiler
Karlheinz Bux
Christoph Freimann
Prof. Paul Isenrath
Gabi Nasfeter
Axel Otterbech
Johannes Pfeiffer
Carlos Ramirez
Prof. Erwin Reiter
Karl Schmid
Hannah Stütz-Menzel

Ulmer Münster
100 Jahre vollendet

inulmurnulmundumulmrum

Mit einem großen, fröhlichen, bunten Fest wollte die Stadt Ulm den 100. Jahrestag der Vollendung ihres berühmten Münsters feiern – drei Wochen lang mit vielen Aktivitäten, mit Konzerten, Ausstellungen, Gottesdiensten, Lichtinstallationen.

Unser visuelles Konzept sollte diese fröhliche Vielfalt und Stimmung zum Ausdruck bringen, sich nicht in einem Logo, Zeichen oder Stempel erschöpfen, es sollte auf das Ulmer Münster verweisen, ohne in einer Postkartenplatitüde zu versinken.

inandaround Ulm

The city of Ulm wanted to celebrate the 100th anniversary of the completion of its famous cathedral with a large, cheerful, colorful festival – three weeks packed with activities, concerts, exhibitions, church services, light installations.

Our visual concept was to express this cheerful diversity and exuberance, not be restricted just to a logo, symbol or stamp; it was to refer to the Ulm Cathedral, without lowering itself to becoming a postcard platitude.

ulm

Within the image:
Stein gewordene Träume

ulm

Münsterfest
11. Mai bis 3. Juni 1990

Ulmer Münster
100 Jahre vollendet

ulm

Ulmer Münster
100 Jahre vollendet

ulm

Wie könnten wir dieses Ulmer Münster, dieses bekannte, vertraute Merk-Mal Ulms über das Gewohnte und Gewöhnliche hinaus sichtbar und interpretierbar machen?

In fast detektivischer Weise näherten wir uns mit der Kamera dem gotischen Bauwerk auf unruhiger Entdeckungsreise nach dem „Besonderem", „Unverwechselbaren", dem alten „Neuen", dem neuen „Alten".

How could we make Ulm Cathedral, this familiar, famous landmark of Ulm, visible and open it up to interpretation beyond the domain of the usual and familiar?

As if we were detectives, we approached the Gothic building with a camera on a restless journey in quest of what makes it "special", "distinct", in search of the old "new", the new "old".

Room to Move **is a beautiful book, celebrating over twenty years of Baumann & Baumann's work.** Most spreads present examples of projects in generous spaces that enable extravagant explorations of the essence of each design, making the book itself just as valuable as the work it contains.

The cover and slip case herald the sophisticated simplicity for which Baumann & Baumann is famous, and we have chosen two of three double-page spreads displaying the designs for Ulm Cathedral's hundredth anniversary as typical of the striking content and composition throughout the book. Sections of the building silhouette are key elements within the items produced for this project. As a consequence, these pages are filled by replications of the positive and negative shapes of the silhouettes. Sometimes the shapes are strong, flat colors; other times they are picture boxes, containing colorful photographs of celebratory events at the cathedral and offering pleasing contrast in texture and rhythm.

DESIGN FIRM **ODED EZER DESIGN
STUDIO** ● DESIGN **ODED EZER** ●
PHOTOGRAPHY **ODED EZER** ● CLIENT
ODED EZER DESIGN ● PROJECT NAME
THE MESSAGE POSTER

Oded Ezer is fond of working in three dimensions. In his poster The Message, he pays typographic homage to the music of the avant-garde composer Arye Shapira by partially cutting out and raising areas of letterforms that make up the titles of Shapira's music. The subsequent photograph of this concept produces a chaotic interplay of image and shadow, reflecting pace, tone, volume, and probable musical instruments. Little information is being communicated, but the size and complexity of the type, perspective view, and cropping not only fill the area, but also provide a sense of expansive space.

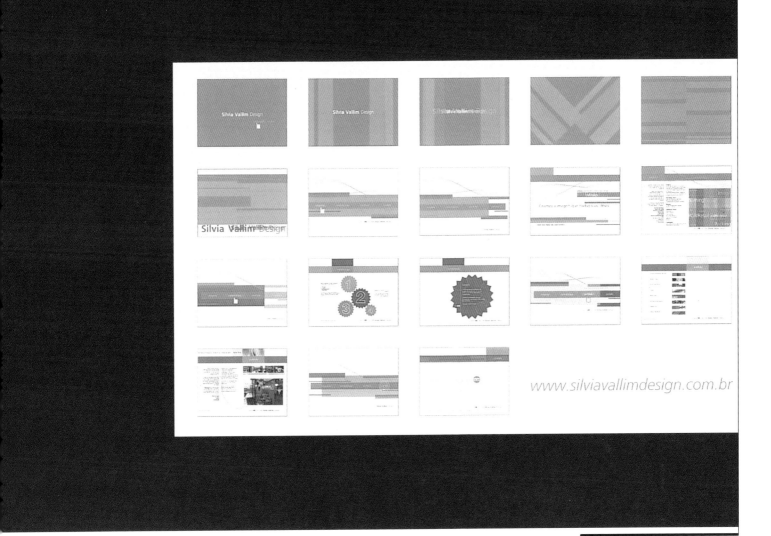

www.silviavallimdesign.com.br

In many respects, this Web site contains quite a lot of information, but we included it in this section because of the pleasing animated sequences that generously explore the greens and linear patterns of Silvia Vallim's identity. From completely green pages to horizontal green slithers interrelating with succinct type and waving, fine, gray lines, the introduction gently leads the viewer to a stylish and fresh homepage. The subsequent repetitive returns to this section make the site airy yet informative.

DESIGN FIRM **SILVIA VALLIM DESIGN** ● ART DIRECTION **SILVIA VALLIM** ● DESIGN **SILVIA VALLIM, BETA MOTTA** ● COPY **SILVIA VALLIM, PEDRO RIBEIRO** ● ILLUSTRATION **SILVIA VALLIM** ● PHOTOGRAPHY **GUSTAVO PASCHOAL, MARCOS VIANNA** ● WEB PRODUCTION **LEONARDO SIMÖES** ● CLIENT **SILVIA VALLIM DESIGN** ● PROJECT NAME **SILVIA VALLIM DESIGN WEB SITE**

Niklaus Troxler clearly has a passion for extremely expressive mark making and composition within his posters, turning his expanses of space into energetic vehicles of meaning.
This wheelchair poster is no exception. Offset, repetitive overlays of linear illustration interact with lines of type replicating angles and line weights. Together with the colors of lime green, orange, and white, the image communicates the impression of speed, force, and intensity within the race itself. Despite the scale of the poster, the image is dramatically cropped, making the message far more arresting.

DESIGN FIRM **NIKLAUS TROXLER**
DESIGN ● DESIGN **NIKLAUS TROXLER**
● ILLUSTRATION **NIKLAUS TROXLER** ● CLIENT **WHEEL CHAIR SCHENKON** ● PROJECT NAME **WHEELCHAIR RACE**

DESIGN FIRM **[I]E DESIGN** ● ART
DIRECTION **MARCIE CARSON** ●
DESIGN **MARCIE CARSON, CYA**
NELSON ● PHOTOGRAPHY **JOHN**
RUBINO ● CLIENT **[I]E DESIGN** ●
PROJECT NAME **[I]E DESIGN**
CAPABILITIES BROCHURE

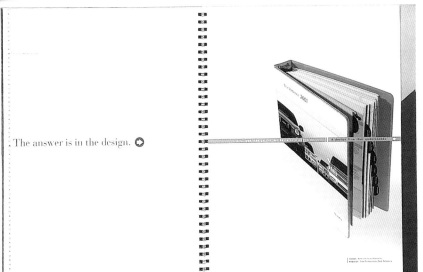

Self-promotion must interest and intrigue the reader instantly. Alli

Neiman of [i]e design comments, "WE FELT THAT IF WE WERE TOO WORDY AND PACKED WITH INFORMATION, OUR BROCHURE WOULD BE THROWN OUT. WE WANTED OUR AUDIENCE TO INTERACT WITH THE PAGES AND ENJOY THE CHANGES IN TEXTURE AND PROCESS."

On the cover and throughout each spread, unexpected combinations of color, material, scale, and technique come together to impress. With very few elements within each composition, the readers' concentration is focused on the detail, free of distractions from gratuitous contents.

Li Zhang uses a large capital *N* together with a lowercase *n* as both image and type to construct this poster for Purdue University. Because these letterforms bleed off the edges, the positive and negative shapes have almost equal importance, and Zhang has treated each area individually, whether part of a letter or counterform. Simple, brightly colored shapes dominate the layout, with vertical and horizontal text visually relating to key alignment points and focal areas.

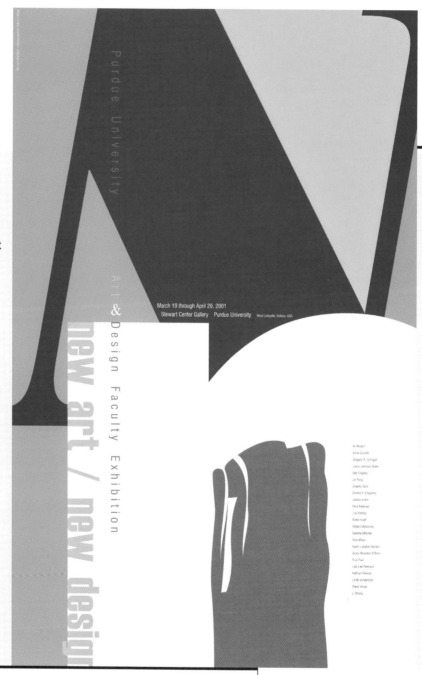

DESIGN FIRM **PURDUE UNIVERSITY** ● DESIGN **LI ZHANG** ● COPY **LI ZHANG** ● CLIENT **PURDUE UNIVERSITY** ● PROJECT NAME **NEW ART/NEW DESIGN**

DESIGN FIRM **TRICKETT & WEBB, LTD.**
● ART DIRECTION **BRIAN WEBB, LYNN TRICKETT** ● DESIGN **BRIAN WEBB, LYNN TRICKETT, KATJA THIELEN** ●
COPY **MICHAEL BENSON** ● CLIENT **CAMBERWELL PRESS** ● PROJECT NAME **1,000 YEARS 1,000 WORDS**

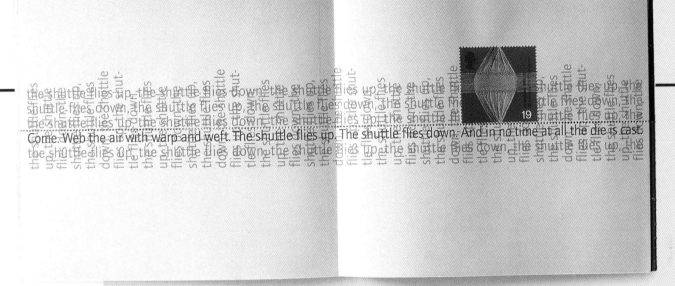

Come. Web the air with warp and weft. The shuttle flies up. The shuttle flies down. And in no time at all the die is cast.

These two spreads are taken from a book that was designed to decoratively celebrate one thousand years of British history through fifty stamps produced by the Royal Mail during the millennium year. The words are by writer Michael Benson, and the stamps illustrated by fifty well-known artists. As Brian Webb comments, "THE TYPOGRAPHY USES THE SPACE ON EACH SPREAD TO ADD TO THE STORY." In both instances, repetitions of words and phrases replicate the processes of weaving and plowing, with the horizontal and vertical orientations representing the warp and weft of weaving, and the diagonal parallel lines echoing the lines on the stamp to emulate plowing.

Taking up five pages, this article in Ikea's *Room* magazine makes dramatic use of black-and-white photography and minimal text. Copy is positioned in small, narrow columns that fit around the main focus of imagery. Cropping and scale are used to great effect, with close-up portraits presenting eyes and noses, plus every hair, wrinkle, and freckle in minute detail. This is an article on genes and what they mean to us; because they define precisely how we look, the designer focused on the physical details of the subjects.

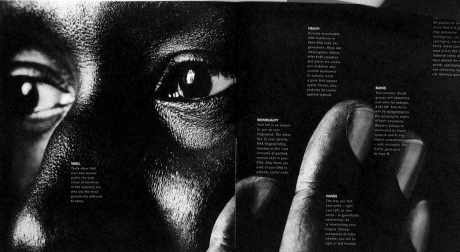

DESIGN FIRM **JOHN BROWN CITRUS PUBLISHING** ● CREATIVE DIRECTION **JEREMY LESLIE** ● PHOTOGRAPHY **LOTTIE DAVIES** ● CLIENT **IKEA** ● PROJECT NAME ***ROOM*, "GENE POOL"**

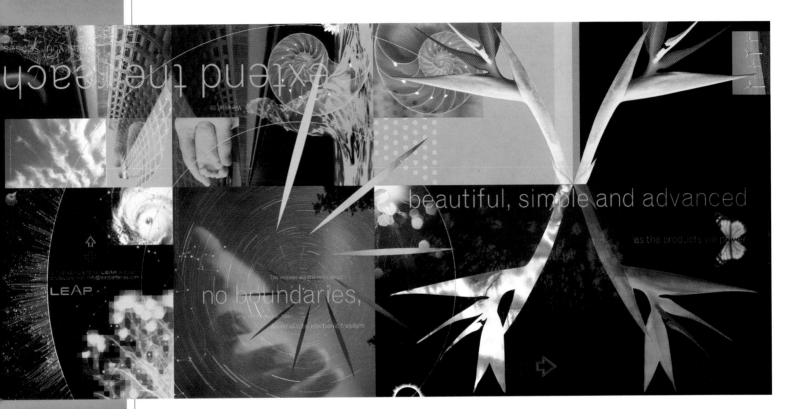

"THE OBJECTIVE WAS TO PRODUCE A FOLDING BROADSHEET WHICH DISCUSSES HOW MODERN BATTERY TECHNOLOGY HAS ENABLED VERY SOPHISTICATED HARDWARE TO BECOME MOBILE AND FREED US TO WORK AND PLAY WHEREVER AND WHENEVER WE WANT," says David Ellis. "WE WANTED TO SET THE SCENE," he continues, "SO WE BEGAN TO THINK OF BATTERIES AS BEING JUST AS SMART AND WELL DESIGNED AS THE PRODUCTS WE USE THEM IN." The complete broadsheet is interestingly filled with squared-up and cut-out fanciful imagery that complements and illustrates the text, producing what Ellis describes as "A COHESIVE AND POETIC WHOLE." The predominantly dark background space helps to bring elements together, while the use of silver ink ensures that all of the text is legible, regardless of background coloring or detail.

DESIGN FIRM **WHY NOT ASSOCIATES**
● COPY **GARY PROUK** ● PHOTOGRAPHY
PHOTODISC, ROCCO REDONDO ●
CLIENT **THE SEBASTIAN
CONSULTANCY** ● PROJECT NAME
LEAP BATTERIES

45

The Owen Roberts Group holiday cards spread season's greetings across seven coasters. Just one coaster extends the company's goodwill, while the other six toy with an eclectic mix of type and imagery, selected with the express need to include a letter *O* (for Owen). "THE STAFF AT OWEN ROBERTS ENJOYS NOTHING MORE THAN HAVING A BIT OF FUN," says Denise Sakaki of Monster Design, "AND WE WANTED TO SHOW THEIR PERSONALITIES IN SOME WAY." The alternative use for so much surface area within this card could ensure a safe coffee mug site for a lot longer than the festive season, and ideally, at least a subliminal awareness of the client!

DESIGN FIRM **MONSTER DESIGN** ●
DESIGN **HANNAH WYGAL, THERESA VERANTH, DENISE SAKAKI** ● CLIENT
OWEN ROBERTS GROUP ● PROJECT
NAME **HOLIDAY COASTER SET**

Nigel Beechey has engineered the AGD NSW 2002 calendar of events to extend across two posters, providing a luxurious amount of space over which to spread the year's events. One side of each poster simply determines which six-month section is being covered through the portrayal of large numerals, "1/2" and "2/2." The other side of each poster is divided into nine equal parts—six for monthly events and three for general association details. Large numerals are perpetuated and the dates and descriptions of events are configured as strong groupings that make varied use of tone and extravagant composition.

DESIGN FIRM **CPD** ● DESIGN **NIGEL BEECHEY** ● COPY **NIGEL BEECHEY** ● CLIENT **AUSTRALIAN GRAPHIC DESIGN ASSOCIATION** ● PROJECT NAME **AGD NSW CALENDAR OF EVENTS**

Bold use of white space complements the unusual intricacies of photography and illustration in these two spreads from an article on fashion. Detailing in the typographic groups, along with complexities of mark making and perspective, are made more prominent through their relationships with the white shapes. Hierarchically, the viewer is drawn to the "empty" areas first, but is then irresistibly led via strong directional lines to the items of clothing featured.

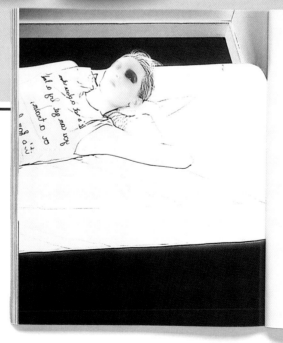

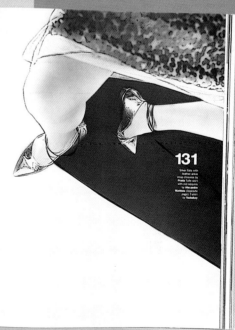

DESIGN FIRM **EXQUISITE CORPORATION** ● ART DIRECTION **RILEY JOHN-DONNELL** ● DESIGN **RILEY JOHN-DONNELL** ● COPY **JEREMY LIN** ● CLIENT *SURFACE* **MAGAZINE** ● PROJECT NAME *SURFACE*, "MAGNETIC FIELD"

One of the things we noted earlier was the power that cutouts have in affecting the space around them. Laurey Bennett's résumé uses the visual excitement of a complex three-dimensional cut-out form to celebrate and enliven its text. Résumés are notoriously predictable, and the extravagant, but intriguing, use of 3-D space adds an unexpected and enticing dimension to this design. Despite the minimal text and lack of color, the viewer is irresistibly drawn into exploring this memorable structure.

DESIGN FIRM **LAUREY ROBIN**
BENNETT DESIGN ● ART DIRECTION
LAUREY BENNETT ● DESIGN **LAUREY**
BENNETT ● CLIENT **LAUREY**
BENNETT ● PROJECT NAME **RÉSUMÉ**

DESIGN FIRM **SCANDINAVIAN DESIGN GROUP** ● ART DIRECTION **MUGGIE RAMADANI, PER MADSEN** ● DESIGN **PER MADSEN, MUGGIE RAMADANI** ● CLIENT **PORTFOLIO-CPH** ● PROJECT NAME **PORTFOLIO-CPH FOLDER AND INFORMATION SHEETS**

"THE CUT-OUT HOLE GIVES PEOPLE THE SENSE OF LOOKING THROUGH THE LENS OF A CAMERA AND, AS SUCH, FORMS AN ICON OR SYMBOL FOR PHOTOGRAPHY, WHICH IS THE CORE PRODUCT OF THE AGENCY," says Muggie Ramadani. The totally plain white cover of the folder becomes a frame for this hole, which cuts right through the different photographers' information sheets inside. Far from appearing as negative space, the simplicity of the white complements the excitement of the cutout. The contrasting blue interior of this folder together with its accurately positioned minimal text produces a similar visual gestalt.

DESIGN FIRM **PING PONG DESIGN**
● COPY **PING PONG DESIGN** ●
ILLUSTRATION **PING PONG DESIGN** ●
PHOTOGRAPHY **PING PONG DESIGN** ●
CLIENT **BUNK ARCHITECTURAL
EVENTS** ● PROJECT NAME **BIG A
POSTER**

One way to win the battle for attention is to move up the ladder of scale. Another one is simplicity. The result is a large amount of space containing very little information, as in the Big A poster created by Ping Pong Design of Rotterdam. From a distance, the huge letter *A* is not only dynamic, "BUT HAS MIGRATED CLOSER TOWARDS ITS SUBJECT MATTER—ARCHITECTURE," says Mirjam Citroen. We think it has a tremendous impact on the surrounding cityscape. The poster promotes a series of opinionated lectures on architecture, urban culture, and city branding as alternatives to the official viewpoint voiced at the Architectuurzomer 2002. Upon closer examination, a second level of information can be accessed in the form of a footnote at the base of the letterform that provides practical information concerning lectures.

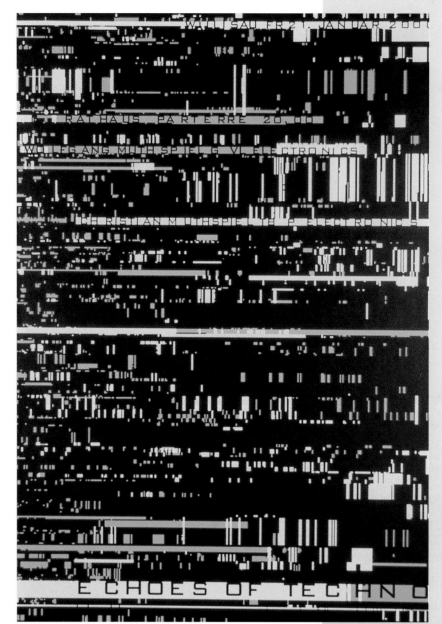

DESIGN FIRM **NIKLAUS TROXLER**
DESIGN ● DESIGN **NIKLAUS TROXLER**
● ILLUSTRATION **NIKLAUS TROXLER**
● CLIENT **JAZZ IN WILLISAU** ●
PROJECT NAME **ECHOES OF TECHNO**

In the introduction to the following section, we compare layout with music, looking at the parallels of different textural and tonal qualities with, for example, volume and pace. Within this poster, Troxler really engages with this principle when he tries to express "THE PROGRAMMED SYSTEMS OF ELECTRONIC TECHNO SOUNDS COMBINED WITH SPONTANEOUS IMPROVISED MUSIC." The message is brief, allowing Troxler to use the space in this large poster (36" × 50.5", 91 cm × 128 cm) to capture the nature of techno in such a way as to enable the viewer to almost "hear" its sounds.

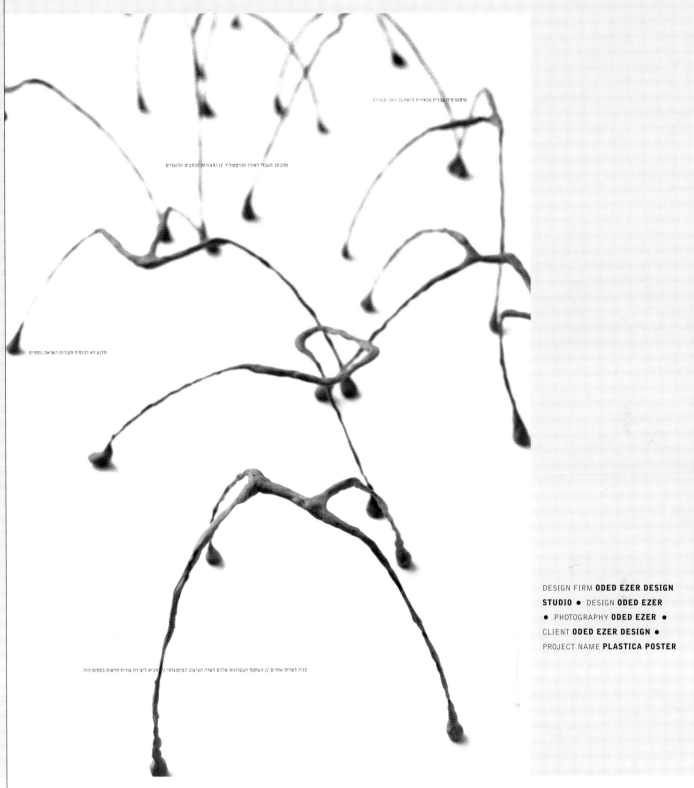

DESIGN FIRM **ODED EZER DESIGN STUDIO** • DESIGN **ODED EZER** • PHOTOGRAPHY **ODED EZER** • CLIENT **ODED EZER DESIGN** • PROJECT NAME **PLASTICA POSTER**

This fascinating typographic poster involves handcrafted Hebrew letterforms that appear to be gathering and moving across the space. As opposed to merely displaying a new font, Oded Ezer experiments with typographic design. His large, almost spider-like creations delicately span the entire poster and are interspersed with lines of small type that expand upon the theme of "designing in a different way." The overall effect is of an extremely airy composition that provides the poster with a light, contemporary feel.

DESIGN FIRM **BAUMANN & BAUMANN**
● CLIENT **SIEMENS AG, MUNICH** ●
PROJECT NAME **SIEMENS IDENTITY**
GUIDELINES

Baumann & Baumann have produced a series of four highly comprehensive and lavish folders that provides information concerning all brand elements of Siemens's identity. Each oversized 11.75" × 8.25" (29.7 cm × 21 cm) pack consists of a foldout container holding a mix of 8.25" × 5.9" (21 cm × 14.8 cm) glossy cards, 33" × 23.5" (84 cm × 59.4 cm) posters, 16.5" × 11.75" (42 cm × 29.5 cm) brochures, and 11.75" × 8.25" (29.7 cm × 21 cm) inserts. Throughout, the extravagant use of space complements precise imagery and text in a manner that enhances the viewers' perception of Siemens's caliber and status. Precision and detailing represent care, professionalism, and reliability, while space suggests quality and availability of time.

On examining the folder more closely, particularly the contents that discuss the Fibonacci sequence and its implications for Siemens's design, it is stimulating to appreciate a series of items that explains and develops the theme in a beautiful and considered manner. Full-color images, accurate line work, type, and mathematical positioning, are partially responsible for this, but it's the generous and carefully positioned space that is most significant in these stylish layouts. The quantity of space allows exciting contrasts of scale, which give the viewer the participatory enjoyment of refocusing from small details to bold enlargements.

Siemens has commissioned its own typefaces, Siemens Sans, Siemens Serif, and Siemens Slab. Another folder in the set is a detailed celebration of all the attributes afforded by these distinctive letterforms, as well as comprehensive instructions on usage. The bright red space on both sides of the folder encompasses minimal text, with large fine outline letters reversed through as image. Inside the folder are five 11.75" × 8.25" (29.7 cm × 21 cm) leaflets in predominantly white, black, and gray, with touches of red. Each has an eight-page foldout that expounds the virtues of every possible curve, angle, weight, and form that contributes to the character of the typeface families. Five glossy 8.25" × 5.9" (21 cm × 14.8 cm) postcards complete the dynamic presentation. As with all the Siemens corporate literature, there is a real sense that time and care that have gone into the design and production of every element. However, it's without a doubt the truly extravagant availability of space that enables the striking compositions, the vast changes of scale and tone, and the sheer pleasure of design for design's sake.

The spacing between the words...

zwischen den Buchstaben...

zwischen den Zeilen...

Abstand

Der Zeilenabstand wird von Schriftlinie zu Schriftlinie gemessen.

... Der Flattersatz hat eine bündige, linke Satzkante und eine offene, auslaufende rechte Satzkante. Der Text ist durch seine gleichbleibenden Wortabstände, dem Grauwert und der Ausgewogenheit besonders gut lesbar.

ROLL OUT (MY BUSINESS

ROLL UP
CLICK TO ENTER

EXCLUSIVE WITH My Village LUDACRIS SOUND
NETWORK

© 2002 Mercury records and made by circus dogs at Holler

DESIGN **FIRM HOLLER** ● DESIGN
JAMES KIRKHAM ● CLIENT
MERCURY RECORDS ● PROJECT
NAME **LUDAPRIZE WEB SITE,**
LUDAPRIZE.COM

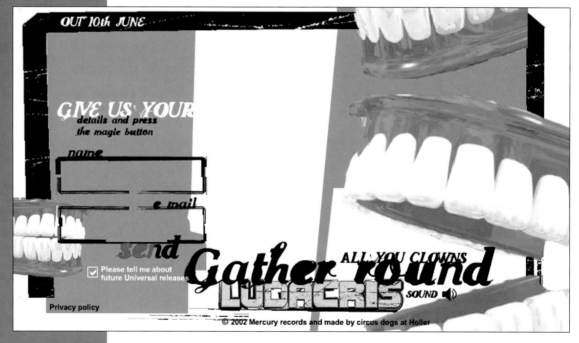

OUT 10th JUNE

GIVE US YOUR
details and press
the magic button

name

e mail

send

☑ Please tell me about
future Universal releases

ALL YOU CLOWNS
Gather round
LUDACRIS SOUND

Privacy policy

© 2002 Mercury records and made by circus dogs at Holler

The animated screens on the Ludaprize Web site are bold and dynamic.
Very little information has to be conveyed to the viewer, and essentially the
compositions are uncomplicated and direct. Visual interest is overtly created
by gnashing teeth and "shouting mouths," but equally significantly, the
distinctive mark making, color changes, typographic groupings, and angles
bring the screen to life and make sense of the spatial distribution.

"WE HAD TO GIVE PEOPLE AN IMMEDIATE SENSE OF THE IMPORTANCE OF PERIPHERE'S FURNITURE, BUT WE HAD VERY LITTLE MATERIAL TO WORK WITH. OUR SOLUTION WAS TO USE A MINIMALIST APPROACH, AND EVOKE RATHER THAN EXPOSE," says Joanne Lefebvre, president of Paprika. The Periphere brochure promotes a new collection of furniture, projecting an image that is high-end, cutting-edge, and established. The client decided on a sixteen-page publication, plus foldout flaps on the front and back covers, but with only a few pieces of furniture in production, Paprika was faced with the difficult challenge of filling it. Carefully positioned elements lead the viewer through the space. On both the cover and the inside foldout spread, very simple pencil scribbles construct movement that leads from and to the image or text within each layout. The photograph on the inside front cover depicts an empty room with a twiglike lamp in the corner. On the next spread, the same room is shown, but with the addition of a chair and one lone, suited male model leaning against the wall. Throughout the catalog, vast areas of white space and black-and-white photographs work together to convey an impression of luxury and style.

DESIGN FIRM **PAPRIKA** ● ART DIRECTION **LOUIS GAGNON** ● DESIGN **LOUIS GAGNON, FRANÇOIS LECLERC** ● PHOTOGRAPHY **RICHARD BERNARDIN, MICHEL TOUCHETTE** ● CLIENT **PERIPHERE** ● PROJECT NAME **PERIPHERE BROCHURE**

DESIGN FIRM **PAPRIKA** ● ART DIRECTION **LOUIS GAGNON** ● DESIGN **LOUISE MAROIS, FRANÇOIS LECLERC** ● CLIENT **BARONET FURNITURE** ● PROJECT NAME **BARONET INVITATION**

In creating a poster and associated invitation for the 2002 High Point Salon, where the client, a high-end furniture manufacturer, was exhibiting their new collection, Paprika came up with seven concepts. The client liked them so much that they requested that all seven be combined in one final solution. "EACH CONCEPT WAS ORIGINATED AS A STAND-ALONE RESPONSE, SO WE DECIDED TO HIGHLIGHT THEIR UNIQUENESS AND TREAT THEM AS A SERIES OF POSTCARDS LINKED IN AN ACCORDION-STYLE FORMAT," says Joanne Lefebvre, of Paprika. "THIS CREATED A VEHICLE THAT WORKED WELL IN MULTIPLES, WITH NUMEROUS CHANGES OF SCALE AND USE." The bottom line is that comparatively little hard information had to be presented, but the concept had a lot of versatility. The poster became a series of posters, which was then turned into invitations, partitions, three-dimensional wallpaper, window displays, and other visually attractive items that had a great deal of impact and power.

A simple and intriguing one-word title, "Threee," is centered on the cover of Hat-Trick's self-promotion. Matte black space frames the shiny, black, debossed letterforms, with three black-ribbon section dividers protruding from the base. The scarcity of visual elements, together with the quality of the processes, creates a "preciousness" that persuades the handler to open the cover and turn the pages gently. Matte black endpapers lead to black-and-white photographs that are organized in luxurious white space, with complete pages of gray and black creating the breaks. The "threee" theme, perpetuated in the content of the images and space, uninterrupted by text, invites readers to author their own captions.

DESIGN FIRM **HAT-TRICK DESIGN** ●
ART DIRECTION **GARETH HOWAT,
DAVID KIMPTON, JIM SUTHERLAND** ●
DESIGN **GARETH HOWAT, DAVID
KIMPTON, JIM SUTHERLAND** ● COPY
LINDSEY CAMP ● PHOTOGRAPHY
**DAVID GIBSON, NICK TURPIN,
MATTHEW STUART** ● CLIENT
HAT-TRICK DESIGN ● PROJECT
NAME **THREEE**

DESIGN FIRM **JOHN BROWN CITRUS PUBLISHING** ● ART DIRECTION **DANIEL BIASATTI** ● DESIGN **SONA HART** ● COPY **SYBIL KAPUR** ● PHOTOGRAPHY **DAVID LOFTUS** ● CLIENT *WAITROSE FOOD ILLUSTRATED* MAGAZINE ● PROJECT NAME *WAITROSE FOOD ILLUSTRATED,* "IN POD WE TRUST"

The pages of *Waitrose Food Illustrated* are packed with fascinating information for anyone keen on eating or cooking. The article "In Pod We Trust" is designed to reflect the quality and reliability of such small vegetables as peas and beans. Space plays a vital role, with generously sized broad serif type and mouthwatering food photography set against spacious, brightly colored backgrounds. The complete commentary runs across seven sides, concentrating the text in just two areas to give a varied pace and fresh interest at every turn of the page.

Paprika has created a striking, space-rich, typographic solution for the labeling of bottled water to be sold exclusively in all Groupe Germain hotels. Each hotel has its own individual identity, and this simple concept enables the design to be appropriate for all. The simplicity has been achieved primarily through lightweight san serif typography and expansive space. Water is one of the purest substances, clear and colorless, and, as a result, is especially suited to this design approach.

DESIGN FIRM **PAPRIKA** ● ART DIRECTION **LOUIS GAGNON** ● DESIGN **FRANCIS TURGEON** ● CLIENT **GROUPE GERMAIN, HÔTEL DOMINION, LE GERMAIN ET GERMAIN DES PRÉS** ● PROJECT NAME **H₂OTEL WATER BOTTLES**

DESIGN FIRM **BELYEA** ● ART
DIRECTION **PATRICIA BELYEA** ●
DESIGN **RON LARS HANSEN** ● COPY
BELYEA ● PHOTOGRAPHY **DAN
TAYLOR, STUDIO 360** ● CLIENT
COLORGRAPHICS ● PROJECT NAME
**SUPER EIGHT ANNOUNCEMENT
BROCHURE**

**This brochure informs designers and art directors of the capabilities of
the first eight-color, full-size press in Washington State.**
"AS BELYEA DETERMINED THE NUMBER OF PAGES," says Patricia
Belyea, "IT WAS CONCEIVED AS AN EXTRAVAGANT PRINT PIECE
WITH MINIMAL COPY AND DRAMATIC USE OF SPACE." The eight-inch
square format, eight-page cover (created by full foldout pages at the front and
back), and eight interior pages are platforms for unusual photographs, subtle
use of varnish and changes of tone, as well as tremendous contrast of scale.
Each spread presents a little more information in a way that makes the
readers' experience unfold in an enjoyable, informative, and untaxing way.

XYLO is an engineering company that develops constructions in wood and, appropriately, beck graphikdesign has chosen a simple wooden cover for this brochure. The inherent characteristics of the plain material enliven the space. Beautiful printing and careful positioning of the logo, combined with a vibrant orange binding, gives credence to the piece. Inside, the orange-and-black theme is perpetuated and the layout draws typographic inspiration as well as image content from the linear nature of the XYLO logo. As if in response to the openness of the cover, the pages contain large-scale photographs, wide landscapes, and heavily leaded type that is as decorative as it is functional.

DESIGN FIRM **BECK GRAPHIKDESIGN**
● ART DIRECTION **KARIN BECK-SÖLLNER** ● DESIGN **KARIN BECK-SÖLLNER** ● COPY **KARIN JENNY** ● PHOTOGRAPHY **WOLFGANG MÜLLER** ● CLIENT **XYLO AG** ●
PROJECT NAME **XYLO BROCHURE**

DESIGN FIRM **JOHN BROWN CITRUS PUBLISHING** ● ART DIRECTION **SIMON ROBINSON** ● DESIGN **CLARE WATTERS** ● COPY **JO SPELLING** ● CLIENT **O MAGAZINE** ● PROJECT NAME **O MAGAZINE, "THE FLYING SCOTSWOMAN"**

the flying scotswoman

When snowboarder Lesley McKenna isn't pulling flat backside 540s (that's somersaults to you and me), she travels all over the world to train. And she always takes her Orange phone along for the ride.

The generous white space in this double-page spread is charged by and, in turn, vitalizes the dynamic grouping of angled type and imagery. All sizes, weights, angles and positions of the content have been meticulously selected to draw the viewer in and through the information. Each element is interrelated, leading the viewer to each piece of information. The introductory paragraph is at the same angle as the head of McKenna, the snowboarder in the large main shot. She appears to be looking at the two-line subhead, creating the ultimate coherence.

KROG's brochure, 12.8" × 9.3" (32 cm × 23 cm), provides generous opportunity for full-color bleed pages of products in order to show craftsmanship and detail. However, this publication has been included in the first section of this book because of the unusual introductory pages dedicated to the different traditional skills featured. In each instance, the designer has allocated a complete spread to create a distinctive visual-verbal gestalt with just a few words and a small amount of simple line work. Powerful type placement results in an image being formed with type. The subsequent layouts reflect enthusiasm and pride in a national heritage.

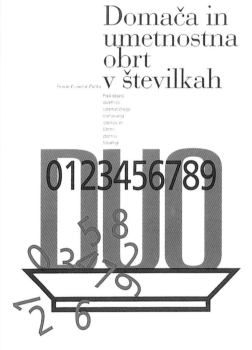

Domača in umetnostna obrt v številkah

0123456789

DESIGN FIRM **KROG** ● DESIGN **EDI BERK** ● COPY **JANEZ BOGATAJ** ● PHOTOGRAPHY **JANEZ PUKSIC** ● CLIENT **OBRTNA ZBORNICA.SLOVENIJE** ● PROJECT NAME **FOURTEENTH EXHIBITION OF FOLK ART IN SLOVENIA**

DESIGN FIRM **RECHORD** ● ART DIRECTION **STEFAN CARTWRIGHT, RACHEL COLLINSON** ● DESIGN **LOUISE CARRIER, RACHEL COLLINSON** ● COPY **TALENT CIRCUS** ● PHOTOGRAPHY **LOUISE CARRIER** ● CLIENT **TALENTCIRCUS** ● PROJECT NAME **TALENTCIRCUS EVOLVING VISUAL IDENTITY, WWW.TALENTCIRCUS.COM**

"ONLINE WE CREATED AN INTERACTIVE SPACE IN WHICH KEY WORDS FLOAT, AND BURSTS OF SOHO LIGHTS CAN BE DIRECTED BY THE AUDIENCE," says Rachel Collinson of Rechord. This concept enables the viewer to select and affect the content and design of the site in an enjoyable participatory manner. Bright colors contrast dramatically with the black background; add to this overlapping words with changes of scale and tone, and Rechord has successfully created a real sense of evolving, animated, three-dimensional space. Much of the visual dynamics are a result of this generous, unfolding, spatial distribution, which is under the control of the viewer's mouse.

DESIGN FIRM **RIPTIDE**
COMMUNICATIONS ● DESIGN **GILL**
BAR-SHAY, YAIR BONEH, YARON
SHAGAL ● PHOTOGRAPHY **NAVE**
COHEN ● CLIENT **THE ISRAELI CIVIL**
RIGHTS SOCIETY ● PROJECT NAME
CIVIL RIGHTS CALENDAR

The use of space is the most significant element within the pages of this Civil Rights calendar. The photographic images are modified by the organization of space around them. In particular, on the page for March, the severe cropping and positioning of the two figures help to convey many nonverbal messages. For example, the space to the right of these figures forces the woman to be almost pushed off the page, emphasizing her diminutive role in relation to the man. Far from being empty, the space powerfully shapes the impact.

DESIGN FIRM **JOHN BROWN CITRUS**
PUBLISHING ● ART DIRECTION
WARREN JACKSON ● PHOTOGRAPHY
ELAINE CONSTANTINE ● CLIENT
VIRGIN ATLANTIC ● PROJECT NAME
HOT AIR, "MEET THE ENTERTAINERS"

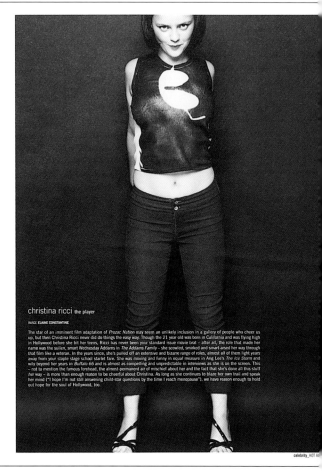

christina ricci the player

IMAGE ELAINE CONSTANTINE

The star of an imminent film adaptation of *Prozac Nation* may seem an unlikely inclusion in a gallery of people who cheer us up, but then Christina Ricci never did do things the easy way. Though the 21 year old was born in California and was flying high in Hollywood before she hit her teens, Ricci has never been your standard issue movie brat – after all, the role that made her name was the sullen, smart Wednesday Addams in *The Addams Family* – she scowled, smirked and smart-arsed her way through that film like a veteran. In the years since, she's pulled off an extensive and bizarre range of roles, almost all of them light years away from your staple stage school starlet fare. She was moving and funny in equal measure in Ang Lee's *The Ice Storm* and wily beyond her years in *Buffalo 66* and is almost as compelling and unpredictable in interviews as she is on the screen. This – not to mention the famous forehead, the almost-permanent air of mischief about her and the fact that she's done all this stuff *her way* – is more than enough reason to be cheerful about Christina. As long as she continues to blaze her own trail and speak her mind ("I hope I'm not still answering child-star questions by the time I reach menopause"), we have reason enough to hold out hope for the soul of Hollywood, too.

celebrity_HOT AIR

OVER THE NEXT 12 PAGES YOU'LL FIND THREE POP STARS, TWO ACTORS, ONE FILM DIRECTOR, AN ARTIST, A DJ – OH – AND ONE BIG SCARY MONSTER. THEY ALL HAVE ONE THING IN COMMON. THEY'VE PUT SMILES ON OUR FACES BY DOING WHAT THEY DO BEST: BEING THEMSELVES.

meet the
entertainers

In order to appeal to its diverse customer base, the Virgin Atlantic magazine, *Hot Air*, offers a broad range of subject matter within its pages.

In the article "Meet the Entertainers," designers have made brave and surprising use of space. Incorporating the informal portraits of twelve artists who are responsible for bringing smiles to our faces, the article takes the reader through wide compacted paragraphs of text, while maintaining the luxury of "acres" of space. The opening spread, shown here, makes dramatic use of contrast, setting the left-hand white page against a full-page portrait of Christina Ricci who poses in dark clothes against a dark background. Open space is also celebrated within titling, grouping copy at the bottom of the page, and justifying text to create exaggerated space between words.

Exhibition spaces can enable large-scale graphics to be used to dramatic effect. Earl Gee notes, "AS PEOPLE IN A TRADE SHOW ENVIRONMENT ARE BOMBARDED WITH MESSAGES, WE CHOSE TO FOCUS ON STRONG, SIMPLE, DIRECT WORDS TO REINFORCE OUR 'INNOVATION' THEME." Single words in fine outline run the full width of each panel and are superimposed on vast, three-dimensional, motorized displays. The silicon wafer products are cleverly utilized as part of a giant flower, a satellite orbiting the Earth, and floating on cloud backgrounds to emphasize the spatial element.

DESIGN FIRM **GEE + CHUNG DESIGN** ●
ART DIRECTION **EARL GEE** ● DESIGN
EARL GEE, FANI CHUNG ● CLIENT
APPLIED MATERIALS ● PROJECT
NAME **APPLIED MATERIALS TRADE
SHOW GRAPHICS**

This double-page spread is an introduction to a strange tale about magnets (among other things!), and in many respects the composition uses the space to visually demonstrate a sense of magnetism. Elements are drawn to one another across the white space, accumulating and grouping toward the right. White type, white counterforms within black letters, and white silhouettes within a photogram manifest the white space in, and through, the spread, with recurring shapes and angles in positive and negative forms acting as "glue."

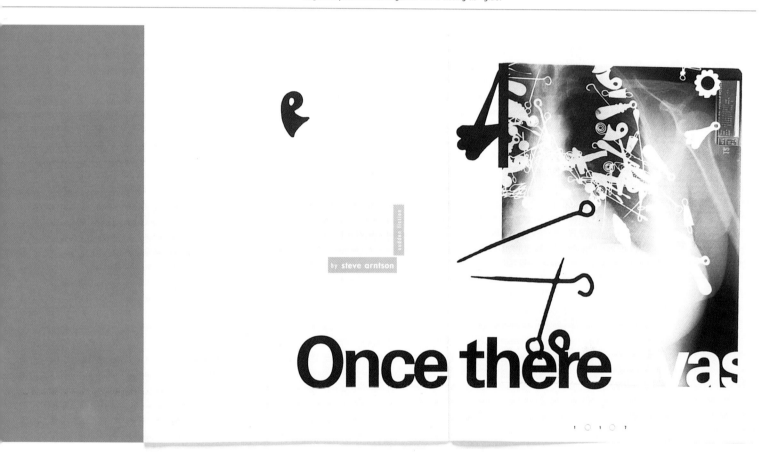

by steve arntson

Once there vas

DESIGN FIRM **APPETITE ENGINEERS**
● DESIGN **MARTIN VENEZKY** ●
CLIENT *SPEAK* **MAGAZINE** ● PROJECT
NAME *SPEAK* **NO. 21**

MAY OCTOBER

BARBICAN INTERNATIONAL THEATRE EVENT

BITE: 01

THEATRE DANCE MUSIC

Box Office
020 7638 8891 (bkg fee)
www.barbican.org.uk

The Barbican is owned, funded and managed by the Corporation of London.

DESIGN FIRM **WHY NOT ASSOCIATES**
● PHOTOGRAPHY **ROCCO REDONDO** ●
CLIENT **THE BARBICAN CENTRE** ●
PROJECT NAME **BITE 01**

The objective of this poster, we are told, was to produce an exciting, energized icon to represent a range of theater events, from dance and performance art to children's puppet shows and everything in between. It was therefore deemed suitable to represent the season of events with simple, generic images. "THE SMALL AMOUNT OF INFORMATION BECAME THE WHOLE FOCUS OF THE DESIGN, BUT RATHER THAN BEING MINIMAL WITH THE LAYOUT, WE BUILT THE WORDS AND USED LIGHTING AND COLOR EFFECTS TO ADD A SENSE OF VIBRANCY AND THEATER TO THE POSTER," says David Ellis.

Space is at the heart of Metalli Lindberg's self-promotion: two-dimensional space on the surface of 7.3" × 4.7" (18.3 cm × 11.7 cm) full-color cards, three-dimensional space in their slotting together to make constructions, and environmental space in terms of the company's relocation to the countryside. Derek Stewart says, "WITH THE INVOLVEMENT OF THE WHOLE STUDIO, WE CREATED AN IDENTITY, BASED ON MATERIAL ELEMENTS, THAT CHARACTERIZED THE SPACE IN WHICH WE WORK AND SHARE."

The invitation to the party celebrating their new location has a wide-open landscape on one side, emphasized by a single line of text spanning the horizon of the grass. "Time to reveal, reopen, refresh, relax," it says, leading the reader to turn over and find "re:" in orange, centered in white space, with the invitation details grouped in a corner. The card has slits cut into all edges, which suggest there must be more to come for building and stacking. Accordingly, a pack of twelve cards was given to everyone at the party, enabling endless individual permutations to be created. Each card expounds the visual-verbal theme, with expanses of color and countryside punctuated by "re" words and a little supporting text. Metalli Lindberg further perpetuated its concept by decorating the party with banners, large projections of the landscape image, and three-dimensional cutout figures.

DESIGN FIRM **METALLI LINDBERG** ●
DESIGN **FRANCESCA SPINAZZÉ,
DEREK STEWART, MARCEL DAL CIN,
JOEL ROBINSON** ● PHOTOGRAPHY
**MARA MAZZANTI, DEREK STEWART,
MARCEL DAL CIN, JOEL ROBINSON** ●
CLIENT **METALLI LINDBERG** ●
PROJECT NAME **SELF-PROMOTIONAL
EVENT**

Guldkorn 2001, a ten-year anniversary book for Danish Advertising and Design, is a superb example of the generous use of space within a design used to connote quality and style. Pages of rich gold and white space, broken only by hairline type and fine geometric illustration, sit alongside full-color pages of Simon Ladefoged's photography of empty rooms and corridors. Both interpretations of open space provide a prestige that influences the viewers' impression of the award-winning work being displayed in the book.

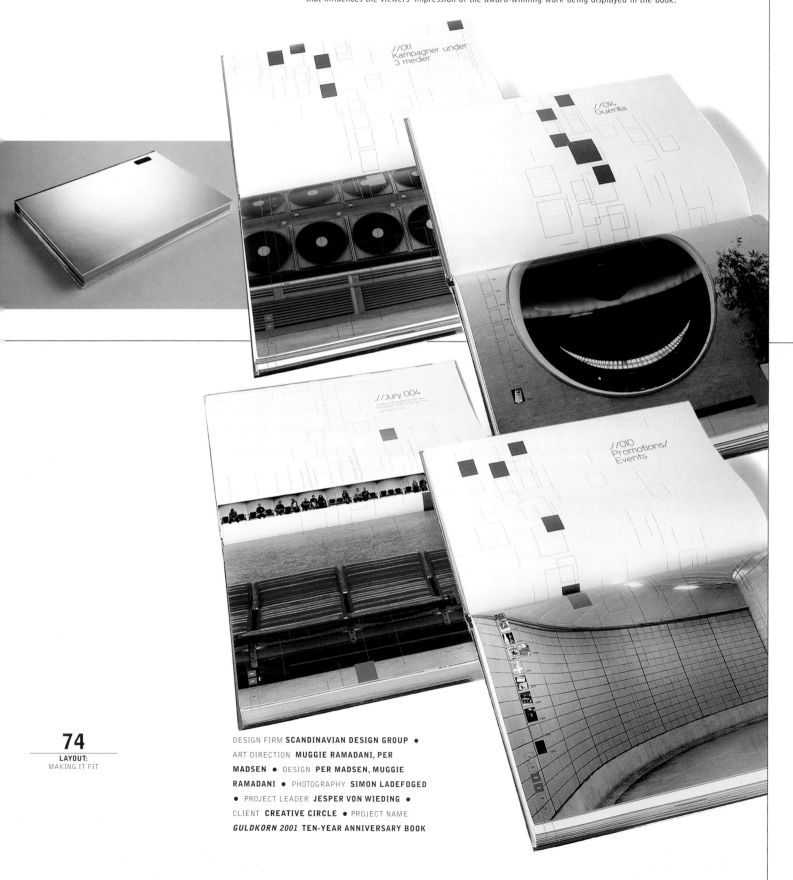

DESIGN FIRM **SCANDINAVIAN DESIGN GROUP** •
ART DIRECTION **MUGGIE RAMADANI, PER
MADSEN** • DESIGN **PER MADSEN, MUGGIE
RAMADANI** • PHOTOGRAPHY **SIMON LADEFOGED**
• PROJECT LEADER **JESPER VON WIEDING** •
CLIENT **CREATIVE CIRCLE** • PROJECT NAME
GULDKORN 2001 **TEN-YEAR ANNIVERSARY BOOK**

Rosemary Butcher Dance Company performances are "AN EXPLORATION OF VIEWS AND PERCEPTIONS OF THE BODY, EXTERNALIZING THE INTERNAL THROUGH LIGHT, IMAGE, AND MOVEMENT," says Rosemary Butcher. As the publicity material needed to reflect this philosophy, x-rays were selected as key elements instead of performance-based imagery. The text is minimal but is used as an integral part of the design, rather than as an explanation or caption. The accompanying invitation was printed on clear plastic and mailed in a clear, glassine bag, which not only perpetuated the dance philosophy, but also took the interpretation of space to new levels, giving every recipient an individual experience and view.

DESIGN FIRM **WHY NOT ASSOCIATES**
● PHOTOGRAPHY **PHOTODISC, DR. HURT** ● CLIENT **ROSEMARY BUTCHER DANCE COMPANY** ● PROJECT NAME **SCAN**

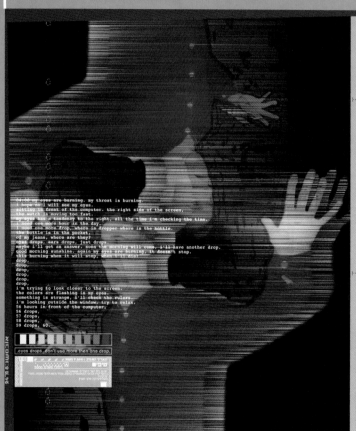

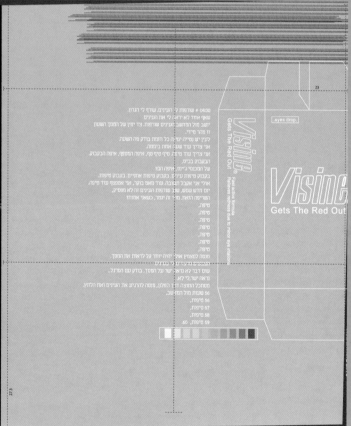

DESIGN FIRM **FREELANCE FOR**
RIPTIDE COMMUNICATIONS ●
DESIGN **GILL BAR-SHAY** ● CLIENT
SELF-PROMOTION ● PROJECT NAME
OBSESSIONS MAGAZINE: DRUGS

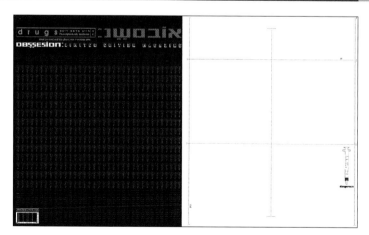

we all do
drug s.

THIS IS AN ADVERTISEMENT

I LOVE MY DRUGS DEALER

קבלת תרופות
רק לפי מרשם

Visual cues in the form of a syringe, a symbolic viper's nest, frantic interplay of type and image, and two distinct headlines identify the topic of these three spreads from *Obsessions* magazine. However, as the reader looks more closely, it is evident that the drugs in question are everyday medicines. Informal configurations and mark making combine to create dynamic and enticing use of space, with the challenge of embracing two languages (Hebrew and English) adding textural diversity. The layouts successfully establish initial ideas, leaving spaces that demand to be filled by the readers' personal interpretations.

munthe plus simonsen

DESIGN FIRM **SCANDINAVIAN DESIGN GROUP** ● ART DIRECTION **MUGGIE RAMADANI, PER MADSEN** ● DESIGN **PER MADSEN, MUGGIE RAMADANI** ● ILLUSTRATOR **CATHRINE RABEN DAVIDSEN** ● CLIENT **MUNTHE PLUS SIMONSEN** ● PROJECT NAME **MUNTHE PLUS SIMONSEN SPRING/SUMMER CATALOGUE 2003**

As one of Denmark's few international trendsetting fashion brands, Munthe plus Simonsen confirms its position as experimental, challenging, and innovative. Scandinavian Design Group has produced a catalog that uses generous amounts of space to define a freedom of spirit and a sense of individuality. The few images of clothing are embellished to give more lifestyle comment than precise detail. Space is filled with panels of textured color and painterly marks that are reminiscent of landscapes, abstract illustration, and interesting fabrics.

DESIGN FIRM **METALLI LINDBERG**
● ART DIRECTION **DEREK STEWART** ●
DESIGN **MARCELLO DAL CIN, JOEL
ROBINSON** ● PHOTOGRAPHY **MILAGRO
STUDIO** ● CLIENT **MOTO GUZZI** ●
PROJECT NAME **NEVADA** 750
PRESS RELEASE

A subtle combination of well-chosen images, clever cropping, and imaginative cutouts increases the impact of this press release by Metalli Linberg. Although the presentation folder and ring-bound catalog are not large in size, the art direction and subsequent cropping of images give this piece a very spacious feel that echoes the impression of speed on the open road. There is very little type to break up the composition, but use of matte finish for the sleeve and gloss for the folder heightens visual interest, as does the contrast of in-focus and out-of-focus photographs.

DESIGN FIRM **SAYLES GRAPHIC
DESIGN** ● DESIGN **JOHN SAYLES**
● ILLUSTRATION **JOHN SAYLES**
● CLIENT **SEATTLE AIGA** ●
PROJECT NAME **DESIGN-O-RAMA
CONFERENCE POSTER**

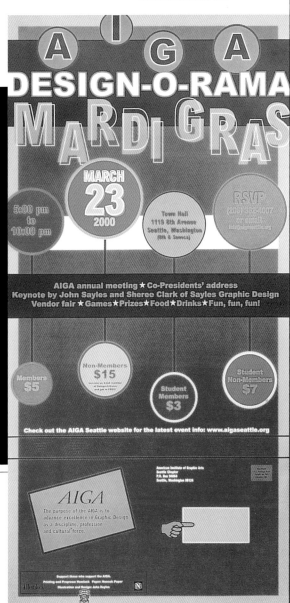

Both the front and back of John Sayles's poster for Design-O-Rama are vibrant compositions of color and pattern. Not a great deal more than who, what, when, and where is present in terms of hard information, leaving the majority of the space to extol the carnival theme of Mardi Gras. Different fonts and sizes of type, geometric shapes, and illustration all jockey for position in a way that replicates John Sayles and Sheree Clark's presentation: "GETTING YOURSELF NOTICED: WE DO IT, AND YOU CAN TOO."

DESIGN FIRM **HAYMARKET PUBLISHING** ● ART DIRECTION **TATIANA OKORIE** ● COPY **COLIN GOODWIN** ● PHOTOGRAPHY **ALEX P** ● REPROGRAPHICS **COLOUR SYSTEMS LONDON** ● CLIENT *JAGUAR MAGAZINE* ● PROJECT NAME *JAGUAR*, "RECORD KEEPER"

> MK VII   > MK VII

record keeper
Funny man Rowan Atkinson has added his own chapter to the history of Jaguar's MkVII racing saloons

38 | Words: COLIN GOODWIN
     Images: ALEX P
                                                            Jaguar | 39

THE PAINT IS FADED IN
PLACES AND LOOKS ALL THE MORE SPLENDID
AND DISTINGUISHED FOR IT

Jaguar didn't build the MkVII as a thoroughbred racer; it was intended primarily as a road car and, as such, it has retained all of the styling points one would expect of a luxury saloon of the early 1950s.

A HUGE PART OF ATKINSON'S
PLEASURE IN OWNING THE MkVII COMES FROM ITS
DEPTH OF HISTORY

Atkinson's car does not have the dividing frame down the centre of the windscreen, which was a characteristic of the type. His uninterrupted vista comes courtesy of a replacement screen off a MkIX.

We were convinced by our very first view of Tatiana Okorie's stunning page for _Jaguar_ magazine that "Record Keeper" should be given a place within this first section. Colin Goodwin's article actually deals with comedian Rowan Atkinson's purchase and addition to the history of a 1951 Jaguar MkVII. Resisting the temptation to feature any shots of this comedy celebrity, Okorie commissioned Alex P to take elegant, almost monochromatic photographs of the car's graceful details. Combining unusual viewpoints with brave cropping and unexpected positioning, pages present this dignified car in large white expanses of space. Typography also has a lightness of touch, with headings and quotes set in the lightest of sans serif type.

Karacters has chosen to utilize the complete surface of the Clearly Canadian bottle to communicate the product details, benefits, and branding. Although this provides a considerable area for imagery and text, designers chose to limit the size, weight, and amount of sans serif type, the color palette, and the variety of pattern. As a result, each bottle is evidence of an exciting synergy of dynamism and simplicity—the former through the strong use of color and effervescent nature of the decoration and the latter through the elongated oval front panel with its minimal information.

DESIGN FIRM **KARACTERS DESIGN GROUP** ● ART DIRECTION **MATTHEW CLARK** ● CLIENT **CLEARLY CANADIAN BEVERAGE CORP.** ● PROJECT NAME **CLEARLY CANADIAN**

"WE TURN HEADS," the copy quietly states on the inside cover of MetroMedia **Technologies' folder**—and this is exactly what the simple but beautifully executed print processes do for this piece. A restrained circular theme is pursued through embossing, debossing, die cutting, and printing on specialist metallic stock, holding the space as positive and active in presenting the quality and prestige of MMT.

A cleverly positioned slit contains MMT's sixteen-page 5.9" × 4.25" (14.8 cm × 10.5 cm) brochure, which continues and echoes the design theme by means of dramatically scaled, cropped, and framed imagery. Moving from page to page through extravagant visual messages, the reader quickly establishes how MMT has become a market leader in its field.

DESIGN FIRM **[I]E DESIGN** ●
ART DIRECTION **MARCIE CARSON** ●
DESIGN **RICHARD HAYNIE, CYA
NELSON** ● CLIENT **METROMEDIA
TECHNOLOGIES** ● PROJECT NAME
**METROMEDIA CAPABILITIES
BROCHURE**

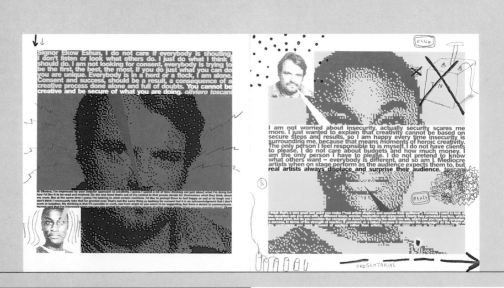

DESIGN FIRM **JOHN BROWN CITRUS PUBLISHING** ● CREATIVE DIRECTION **JEREMY LESLIE** ● COPY **EKOW ESHUN** ● CLIENT **M-REAL** MAGAZINE ● PROJECT NAME **M-REAL**, "**HEAD TO HEAD**"

Dealing with the topic of "response," *M-Real* talks to Oliviero Toscani, someone who has provoked considerable, if not always approving, response to his work.

Within the pages of "Head to Head," the informal, almost graffiti-like nature of illustration and the use of color and of space challenge the reader. Ekow Eshun's discussion with the man most famous for increasing our awareness of the Benetton brand is presented using bright, clashing colors and large, bold type. Appropriately, this article does not shy away from controversy by obliterating many of the pixilated portraits of the interviewer and interviewee— eyes are covered, so are mouths, and finally, on the penultimate page, the whole "illustration" is hidden behind a wall of vast pink type.

Clearly, the DJ Mark B Web site is intent on capturing an ambience that matches the subtle and introspective nature of the musician. It is consequently unusual in that it extravagantly allows much of the screen to be focused on image and mood. Katya Lyumkis says, "WITH LIMITED INFORMATION AND SUBSTANTIAL SPACE AVAILABLE, WE DECIDED TO COMPRESS THE USABLE, INTERACTIVE SECTION OF THE SCREEN INTO A COMPARATIVELY SMALL AREA." Two broad, concentric bands of earthy colors cover more than half the site window, forcing the viewer into the center where tones of deep red configure in semiabstract illustration. A limited amount of partially transparent white text overlays in places, and a white-bordered square identifies the usable location.

DESIGN FIRM **SK VISUAL** ●
ART DIRECTION **KATYA LYUMKIS,**
SPENCER LU ● DESIGN **SPENCER LU**
● CLIENT **DJ MARK B** ● PROJECT
NAME **DJ MARK B WEB SITE**

DESIGN FIRM **FISHTEN** • ART DIRECTION **GILES WOODWARD, KELLY HARTMAN** • DESIGN **GILES WOODWARD, KELLY HARTMAN** • COPY **JOANNE MARION** • CLIENT **MEDICINE HAT MUSEUM AND ART GALLERY** • PROJECT NAME **PHOTO ROMAN**

Pages and pages of green space provide contrast and a passing of time between the photo-based work of the six artists featured in this perfect-bound brochure. To emulate the view through the camera's lens, a strategically positioned small hole cuts through the double thickness of each green page. Giles Woodward of Fishten comments that this extravagant use of space "IS USED TO COMMUNICATE THE PUBLICATION'S INTENTIONS IN A DELIBERATELY FRAGMENTED WAY, TO ENLIGHTEN THE VIEWER A PAGE AT A TIME." Intense colors and a simple L-shaped framing device that is used on the cover and then throughout add to this unusual concept.

After a particularly busy period, Philip Fass took the inspiration for the University of Northern Iowa Gallery of Art Faculty Exhibition Announcement from his desire for "pause" and thought. The central photographic images featuring roads speeding by represent the pace of life and contrast with the expansive white space, signifying contemplation and slow-down. The date information, event announcement, and scheduling are presented and orientated individually, and then bound together by a simple, three-column grid system and two balanced areas of white space.

October 30 through
November 22, 2000

University of Northern Iowa   Department of Art   Faculty Exhibition

OPENING RECEPTION

Kamerick Art Building
Monday, October 30   7:00 PM

gallery hours: Monday through Thursday, 9:00 AM to 9:00 PM
Friday, 9:00 AM to 5:00 PM
Saturday and Sunday, 12:00 PM to 5:00 PM
for more information, contact the gallery at 319.273.3095;
email: gallery@artdept.uni.edu
website: www.uni.edu/artdept/gallery

DESIGN FIRM **PHILIP FASS** ● DESIGN **PHILIP FASS** ● PHOTOGRAPHY **PHILIP FASS** ● CLIENT **UNIVERSITY OF NORTHERN IOWA GALLERY OF ART** ● PROJECT NAME **2000 FACULTY EXHIBITION ANNOUNCEMENT**

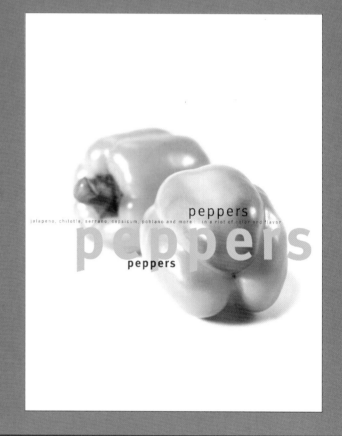

The *Peppers* and *Onions* book jackets bravely allow a generous amount of white space to occupy the covers. The starting position for both image and text has been carefully selected to coincide with the center of the page, creating interesting spaces around this main focus and, says Paul Burgess, "AVOIDING AWKWARD HOLES IN THE LAYOUT."

DESIGN FIRM **WILSON HARVEY** ●
DESIGN **PAUL BURGESS** ● CLIENT
QUINTET ● PROJECT NAME *PEPPERS*
AND *ONIONS* **BOOK JACKETS**

These pages from the Sony site provide small, easy-to-digest chunks of information in a stylish synthesis of image and text.

There is an intrinsic awareness of space, but in each context it is cleverly coordinated through repetitive graphics such as circles, arcs, and transparent overlays, as well as a brave use of the edges of the screen. In particular, the tinted background shapes define the compositions and anchor all elements in relation to them.

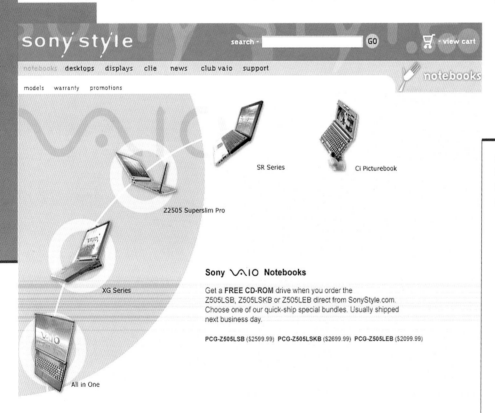

DESIGN FIRM **RIPTIDE COMMUNICATIONS** ● DESIGN **DAVE PAPWORTH** ● CLIENT **SONY** ● PROJECT NAME **SONY VAIO ONLINE**

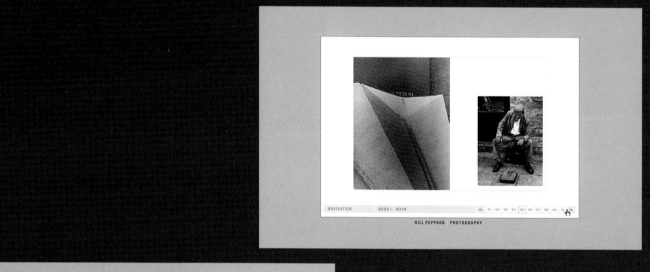

As this is a portfolio site, the primary focus is the photography.

"A CLEAN, SIMPLE, MINIMALIST STATE OF MIND WAS THE MOST LOGICAL," says Paul Flemming of Red Communications, "AND THE FIRST THING WE DID WAS TO 'BLOW OUT' THE WINDOW TO FILL THE SCREEN, HIDING ALL DESKTOP ICONS, AND GIVING AN ELEGANT BROAD GRAY BORDER TO EACH PAGE." Elegance, however, requires the designer to control the resulting space in such a way as to ensure it does not appear empty or bland. The success of the layouts is undoubtedly due to the superb attention to detail—the soft, unobtrusive colors of backgrounds and texts, the contrasts of scale and changes of rhythm, together with the consistency of styling.

DESIGN FIRM **RED COMMUNICATIONS /CREATIVE HOUSE** ● CREATIVE DIRECTION **RICHARD CARMICHAEL** ● DESIGN **PAUL FLEMMING** ● PRODUCTION **PADRIN KWOK** ● PHOTOGRAPHY **HILL PEPPARD** ● CLIENT **HILL PEPPARD** ● PROJECT NAME **HILL PEPPARD WEB SITE, HILLPEPPARD.COM**

The Ecole Buissonnière School has traditionally produced a series of fact sheets for students, including an 8" × 11" (20 cm × 28 cm) photograph of each child. This delightful flipbook, based on traditional animation techniques, provides an engaging and enjoyable alternative. "WE WANTED THE CHILDREN TO ENJOY THIS DOCUMENT AND USE IT," says Joanne Lefebvre of Paprika. Paprika has condensed the original information and format; the booklet is only 2" × 4" (5 cm × 10 cm), making it easier to consult. However, proportionally it achieves the effect of spaciousness. The orientation and grouping of the type leaves plenty of white space to complement the facing bleed photographs, and because each child was shot while jumping up and down on a trampoline, with the camera in a fixed position, there is an impression of continuity and integration. "FLIPPING RAPIDLY THROUGH THE BOOK CREATES THE EFFECT OF MOTION UP AND DOWN, BACKWARDS AND FORWARDS," says Lefebvre. "IT WAS EASY TO CONSULT; STUDENTS LOVED IT, AND WERE HAPPY TO KEEP IT," she continues, "AND THE PROJECT WENT ON TO WIN AN AWARD FROM THE PRESTIGIOUS ART DIRECTORS CLUB OF NEW YORK."

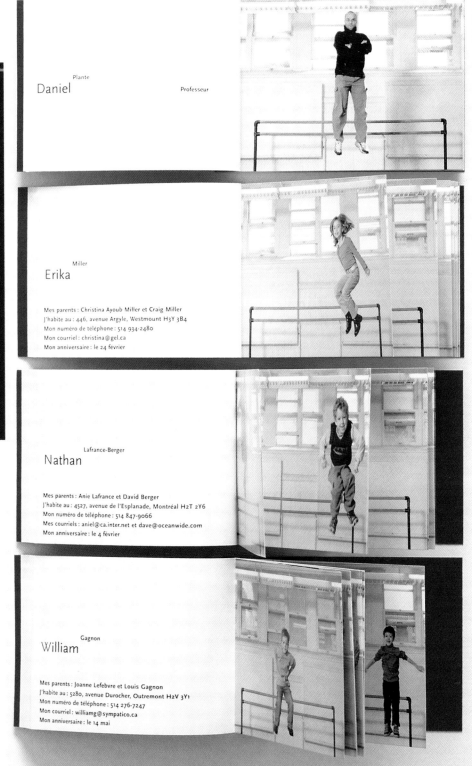

DESIGN FIRM **PAPRIKA** ● ART DIRECTION **LOUIS GAGNON** ● DESIGN **RENÉ CLÉMENT** ● CLIENT **ECOLE BUISSONNIÈRE** ● PROJECT NAME **ECOLE BUISSONNIÈRE BOOKLET**

Vil du være med til at gøre en forskel...

Vi søger mennesker, der både kan og vil noget med deres karriere og liv.
Mennesker, der tager kritisk og konstruktiv stilling til firmaet og til deres egen rolle,
og vil engagere sig i at gøre en forskel. Som forlanger forandringer og som viser, at de
hurtigt kan finde kernen i en problemstilling og har lyst til at løse den. Det er ikke kun
din teoretiske baggrund, som er afgørende. Personlige egenskaber vejer også tungt,
ligesom du naturligvis skal have lyst til at leve efter vores værdier og til at arbejde som
en selvstændig, individuel teamworker. Og så har du sikkert en relevant uddannelse eller
en anden interessant baggrund, som vores kunder kan få glæde af.

Få flere detaljer på www.pwc.dk/recruit

"THE TYPICAL ATTITUDE TOWARDS THE 'ACCOUNTING WORLD' IS THAT IT IS VERY BORING AND CLICHÉD," says **Muggie Ramadani of the Scandinavian Design Group,** "AND THE PURPOSE OF THIS BROCHURE IS TO COUNTER THAT." Instead of including the predictable comprehensive copy and numerous case study images, the twenty-two pages of this publication present atmosphere and image, with comparatively little information. Eight double-page spreads are taken up with generous all over bleed photographs, giving a very honest, documentary feel of a variety of different businesses, with only a brief paragraph of text reversed through on one side. Simple changes in scale and focal distance create variety of pace and rhythm, and consistency within the color palette maintains continuity. The brown wrapping-paper style cover and endpapers are printed with the names of all the company's employees in Denmark in a clear varnish to celebrate the company's most important asset.

DESIGN FIRM **SCANDINAVIAN DESIGN GROUP** ● DESIGN **MUGGIE RAMADANI** ● COPY **SIGNE DUUS** ● PHOTOGRAPHY **SIMON LADEFOGED** ● CLIENT **PRICE WATERHOUSE COOPERS** ● PROJECT NAME **PRICE WATERHOUSE COOPERS IMAGE BROCHURE**

"Godt med lidt frisk luft til hjernen..."

kl. 16:14 - Kenneth Wallin fra København tager sig en mental pause og reflekterer over dagens udfordringer.

Du bliver aldrig for klog til at lære noget nyt

Vi lever af at sælge viden. Derfor prioriterer vi din videnopbygning og videnfastholdelse meget højt. Gennem vores omfattende og grundlæggende uddannelsesprogram klæder vi dig på til præcis den rolle, det ansvar og de arbejdsopgaver, som du får. Ovenpå dette kan du sammensætte et uddannelsesforløb, der tager højde for dine individuelle ønsker. Din uddannelse sker også i det daglige, hvor både danske og internationale opgaver og projekter giver dig mulighed for at suge til dig af praktiske erfaringer. Samtidig har du altid mulighed for coaching og sparring med garvede kolleger. Mange af dem er i dig selv markante personligheder, der besidder en viden på netop deres felt, som du let kan trække på. Du skal selvfølgelig også selv videregive og formidle viden, bl.a. via interne og eksterne artikler, så du bidrager aktivt til, at vores mange videndatabaser er opdaterede.

Se mere på www.pwc.dk/uddannelse

95

DESIGN FIRM **IDENTIKAL** ● DESIGN
NICK HAYES, ADAM HAYES ● CLIENT
T26 ● PROJECT NAME
T26 NEWSPAPER

The typefaces designed by Identikal embody a style that doesn't just come from the character of the letterforms, but is engendered in the overall presentation of the newspaper. The newspaper has twenty pages displaying sixteen different families of type, which are shown in a very personalized way. Nick and Adam Hayes often use the majority of the space on a page to create decorative illustrations that pick up on distinctive recurring letter shapes. Although it seems as if a lot is going on, not much information is being conveyed in this fairly weighty piece. It is predominantly the choices of color, patterning, and composition, which are typical of Identikal, that are used to affect one's perception of the fonts.

Another packaging line that Metalli Lindberg has designed for Ecor SpA is for four different flavors of crackers. Once again, the concept is striking and uncluttered, making the packages stand out from the majority. Instead of detailed product shots, name styles, captions, and descriptions dominating the surfaces, carefully selected visual cues simply and distinctively carry the intended messages. The aluminum bag containers remind the purchasers of quality crisps and chips. The lightweight, minimal sans serif type on the labels hint of a special care and consideration in the production. The color coding combined with clean, fresh illustrations and a squared-up, geometric composition all amalgamate to suggest a quality snack food.

DESIGN FIRM **METALLI LINDBERG** ● ART DIRECTION **DEREK STEWART** ● DESIGN **FRANCESCA SPINAZZÉ** ● ILLUSTRATION **FRANCESCA SPINAZZÉ** ● CLIENT **ECOR SPA** ● PROJECT NAME **ECOR CRACKERS PACKAGE DESIGN**

DESIGN FIRM **HAYMARKET PUBLISHING** ● ART DIRECTION **BEN MARTIN** ● COPY **OLIVER PEAGAM** ● PHOTOGRAPHY **CLIVE ROSE, JAMES MITCHELL** ● REPROGRAPHIC **COLOUR SYSTEMS LONDON** ● CLIENT **TOYOTA** ● PROJECT NAME ***ONE AIM,* "MISSION CONTROL"**

"Mission Control" is the title for the article presenting Panasonic Toyota Racing's Motor Homes. Taking up six pages within the Toyota magazine *One Aim*, this feature elegantly demonstrates the art of designing with limited information in a generous amount of space.

Ben Martin has directed and selected powerful photography that tells the story of these remarkable vehicles. Both imagery and text make dynamic use of contrast of scale. The large images of interiors are paired with smaller views of stylishly furnished detail, while Oliver Peagam's copy, in light gray, is quietly placed to explain the function of this innovative vehicle's spaces. The designers have not only truly succeeded in spreading the content over six pages in a balanced and meaningful way, but also their clean and linear concept echoes that of the ultramodern vehicles in both style and color palette.

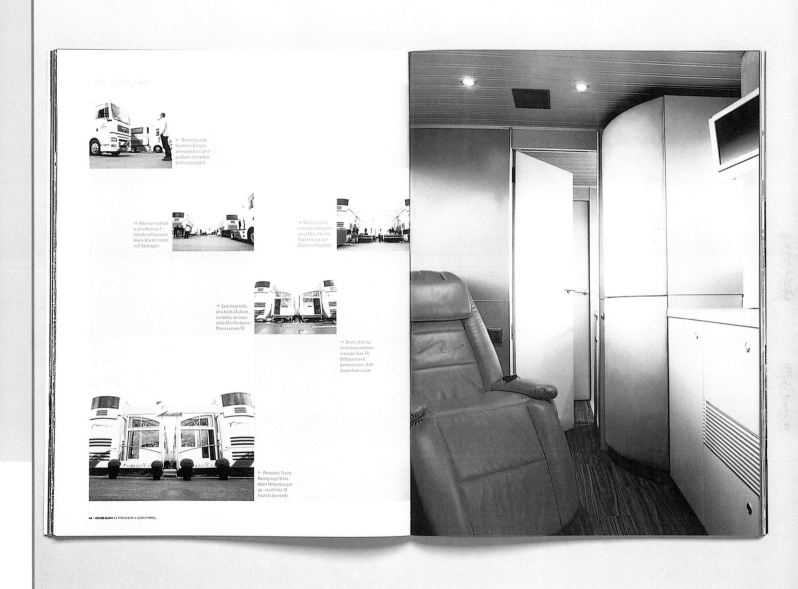

← The trailer units, fresh from Cologne, are reversed into their paddock slot six days before a grand prix

→ Attention to detail is all in Formula 1 – note the yellow spirit levels. One millimetre out? Start again

→ The hospitality units are put together using 10 roof beams, 16 panels and over 20 connecting struts

→ Each hospitality area holds 24 chairs, six tables, six vases and a 42in Panasonic Plasma screen TV

→ Driver' chill-out rooms have a shower, massage chair, TV, DVD player and games console. Both drivers have a room

← Panasonic Toyota Racing is go! It has taken 16 hours to put up – it will take 16 hours to dismantle

The title sequence for the program about Louis Theroux's travels around the world is predominantly pictorial. "WE CHOSE TO DESIGN THE SEQUENCE AS IF IT WAS A LONG PANNING SHOT OVER LOTS OF 'WINDOWS,'" says Jean Cramond, "SHOWING LOUIS INTERACTING WITH SPACIOUS TRAVEL ILLUSTRATIONS AND LIVE ACTION SHOTS FROM THE SERIES." The result is vibrant, large-scale patterns representing environments that dynamically contrast with silhouettes of Louis, and butt up to complementary black-and-white photographs to create powerful and arresting visual relationships.

DESIGN FIRM **BBC DESIGN BRISTOL**
● DESIGN **JEAN CRAMOND** ● CLIENT
ABSOLUTELY PRODUCTIONS ●
PROJECT NAME **WEIRD WEEKENDS**
SERIES 3

Photographed by Peter Guenzel # Drive # By

Stockley Park Golf Club in Middlesex & **Prince's Golf Club** on the Kent coast.
Both a public example of a golf's departure of the past.

B

Golf courses are viewed up close in terms of their design and beauty, seen in terms that are a serious element also completely penetrating. Drive primarily focuses side and geographical positions of the area in which they enjoy is located.

Prince is welcomed in the superior for its overwhelming style of golfed links made by a select group of wealthy individuals back in 1906 and a tremendous research meeting if the course which awoke the grasses and was developed of the landing a couple of holes in Kent's estuarial forest filled with mud then the view's standing more was required.

Prince is at best left, which shows was designed with the potential for surplus in mind. The course project but cut off free and dry uniform or the form painting with and the much refreshingly such.

Its major features are the natural that each clubhouse both in seal for low or of both appears much only the view of this and the horizons. They are used to locate the overstuff range of the face and weigh, of course, but the grounds conclude are still used to earthen penalties for this energy.

A comparison that if we wish to see the grass distinguish of only interrupted by the arrival if the sea the watching if the dull grass and the ones lengthening their way towards the client activity and the scene with a golf.

A course such as Prince's almost certainly couldn't be built anywhere in Europe now, such are the restrictions on environmentally sensitive areas or sites of special scientific interest - which nearly all coastal regions have become. so much this a golf of the if whole slope for design is a long a one in the developments but around the fairly of the old they the world was also.

Prince's is the traditional club can be to indicate a leadership, built to order links land by a small group of wealthy individuals back in 1906.

DESIGN FIRM **MEDIA CELL** ● DESIGN
MICKEY BOY G ● CLIENT **BOGEY
MAGAZINE** ● PROJECT NAME **BOGEY,
"DRIVE BY"**

The "Drive By" article consists mainly of images that explore the differences between an "old school" golf course and a recently built course on a landfill site. Photographs sit side by side with their frames and horizons positioned at the same levels across the five pages. "THE EDITORIAL IS PHOTO LED," says Mickey Boy G, "AND COPY IS INTRODUCED AS EMBELLISHMENT, RATHER THAN A DISTRACTION." It is the unusual way in which smaller shots are dropped into asymmetrical cutaway sections that becomes the focus of attention. The layout uses subtle yet unexpected changes of typographic weight and scale and especially surprises the viewer as one golf course changes to another, distinguished primarily by differing skies.

DESIGN FIRM **DIGITAL VISION ART DEPARTMENT** ● DESIGN **DARREN HUGHES** ● COPY **PAUL NESBIT** ● PHOTOGRAPHY **MAX OPENHEIM** ● CLIENT **DIGITAL VISION** ● PROJECT NAME **VIE LIFESTYLE CATALOGUE**

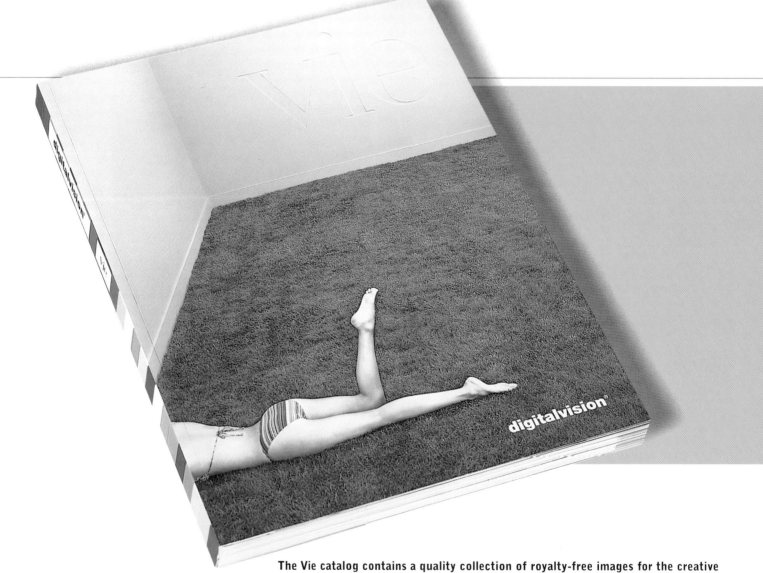

The Vie catalog contains a quality collection of royalty-free images for the creative community. For its very first cover design, Darren Hughes has chosen to capture the essence of the new and exciting contents, inspiration, and imagination. The synergy of expansive photographic and design layout space engineers an intriguing and dynamic hierarchy, leading the viewer from the bikini-clad bottom along one leg to "digitalvision," and then along the other leg up to an embossed "vie." Less overtly, however, the height of visual stimulation comes from the brightly colored bikini stripes "becoming" giant horizontal lines that run across the spine and around onto the whole of the back.

DESIGN FIRM **Y+R 2.1** ● DESIGN **CHRIS ROONEY** ● COPY **CHRIS ROONEY** ● PHOTOGRAPHY **THOM WENTZEL** ● CLIENT **THE YOUNG AND RUBICAN GROUP, SAN FRANCISCO** ● PROJECT NAME **INVITATION TO AN EVENING AT LE COLONIAL**

This invitation to a client appreciation event has been allocated to section one because, strictly speaking, it is only required to include the usual invite material of date, place, time, and so on. However, Chris Rooney of Y+R 2.1 has chosen to encompass these details in an extravagant package of items that evoke the nationality and era of the venue. "INVITEES WERE TAKEN BACK IN TIME TO ANOTHER WORLD WHEN THEY RECEIVED THE INVITATION CONTAINING ILLUSTRATED DIRECTIONS TO THE EVENT, A HAND-STAMPED, LETTERPRESS PASSPORT, AND A RESPONSE CARD DISPLAYING ACTUAL CURRENCY OF THE PERIOD," says Rooney. Unlike many replica concepts that result in a rather wasteful use of time and (paper) space, this piece is a pleasing celebration of attention to design detail and use of appropriate processes.

The second section of this book examines selected examples of work that rise to the challenge of dealing with large amounts of information in limited spaces. This does not mean that the spaces need necessarily be small, but that relative to the area available, a lot of content must be included. The initial reaction to a project that demands the inclusion of considerable text and imagery is often one of dread. How is everything going to fit in, and will it be possible to achieve sufficient visual interest? There is no doubt that this situation can be daunting, but in reality it can be a helpful starting point. It could even be argued that the inclusion of more information provides designers with plenty of material to manipulate and, as a consequence, the opportunity to produce a great variety of successful layouts.

Our examples in this section come from an amazingly wide variety of projects. We have even included

STRONGLY SATURATED AND 'SOFT' COLORS, OR CONTRAST BETWEEN RED AND BLUE), AND PLACEMENT IN THE VISUAL FIELD."

DESIGN FIRM **WILSON HARVEY** ● ART DIRECTION **PAUL BURGESS** ● DESIGN **STEPHANE HARRISON** ● CLIENT **SOPHRON PARTNERS** ● PROJECT NAME **SOPHRON CASE STUDIES**

THE DESIGNER'S dread?

newspaper spreads that, in our opinion, are beautifully designed and on a number of counts break traditional expectations. In an increasingly visually literate world, it seems that the vernacular of news and current affairs is taking on style.

From a practical point of view, quantities of information are generally broken down into different hierarchical levels. Each level can then be given a different visual treatment, and the viewer is led through the design in a particular sequence. If these levels are perceived as categories of texture and tone, whether all type, all image, or a combination of both, the reader will go to the most distinct textures and the darkest tones first, then systematically progress through less prominent textures and lighter tones. A layout that is organized hierarchically is not only more meaningful, but it is also far more visually stimulating and memorable for the viewer.

Kress and Leeuwen reinforce this in *Reading Images: The Grammar of Visual Design* when they say, "THE VIEWERS OF SPATIAL COMPOSITIONS ARE INTUITIVELY ABLE TO JUDGE THE 'WEIGHT' OF THE VARIOUS ELEMENTS OF COMPOSITION, AND THE GREATER WEIGHT OF AN ELEMENT, THE GREATER ITS SALIENCE. THIS SALIENCE, AGAIN, IS NOT OBJECTIVELY MEASURABLE, BUT RESULTS FROM COMPLEX INTERACTION, A COMPLEX TRADING-OFF RELATIONSHIP BETWEEN A NUMBER OF FACTORS: SIZE, SHARPNESS OF FOCUS, TONAL CONTRASTS (FOR INSTANCE THE CONTRAST BETWEEN

Wilson Harvey's Sophron Case Studies is a good example of how simple changes in typographic texture and tone can be used to control the hierarchy. Changes of weight, color, and scale provide different degrees of prominence and meaning and lead the reader through this information.

"THE KEY WAS TO BREAK THE INFORMATION DOWN," says Paul Burgess, "AND COMMUNICATE IN MANAGEABLE CHUNKS, SO AS TO AVOID BOMBARDING THE READER WITH AN INFORMATION OVERLOAD." By making this very wordy piece purely typographic, Wilson Harvey has retained space throughout, using varieties of texture, tone, and color to create interest.

Effective design, whether consciously or unconsciously produced, is often the result of quite systematic processes. Gyorgy Kepes in Language of Vision describes a number of practical theories on the power of organizing space—how space can control the visual hierarchy and visual language, and, in turn, how this can affect the verbal language. He tells us, "SPATIAL ORGANIZATION IS THE VITAL FACTOR IN AN OPTICAL MESSAGE…IN THE FIELD OF VISUAL EXPERIENCE, THE PROXIMITY OR SIMILARITY OF OPTICAL UNITS IS THE SIMPLEST CONDITION FOR A CRYSTALLIZATION OF UNIFIED VISUAL WHOLES."

Kepes considers three main influences on visual sequencing, which he categorizes as proximity, similarity, and continuance. Proximity is the close positioning of elements, which encourages them to be read together. Despite visual differences of scale, shape, or style, the surrounding space will hold items together as meanings to be related. Similarity is the linking of elements purely by their similar appearance. The viewer will go from one to the other regardless of orientation or position, ignoring components that are visually different. Continuance leads the reader visually from one image to another in a comparatively linear fashion, using space to define the composition.

Managing complex quantities of information, especially within limited spaces, is an exciting challenge that calls for resourcefulness and a heightened awareness of visual rhythms. Layouts can often be paralleled with music. Variations on themes, pace, volume, and mood can be replicated through use of color, composition, scale, and weight, and while looking at different layouts, it can be beneficial to imagine their musical interpretation. Layouts that involve dynamic changes of scale, weight, and color can be 'heard' as music that involves great variety in volume, pitch, and pace.

DESIGN FIRM **ROUNDEL** ● ART
DIRECTION **MICHAEL DENNY** ●
DESIGN **STEVE PARKER** ● CLIENT
KOWLOON–CANTON RAILWAY ●
PROJECT NAME **KCR PICTOGRAM
SIGNS**

Designs that use the same degree of detailed attention, but have more subtle textural and tonal changes, can 'sound' as if they have less diversity of pitch and more regularity of tempo and volume. As Philip B. Meggs says in *Type and Image: The Language of Graphic Design*, "ANOTHER ASPECT OF THE DESIGNER'S TASK IS TO INFUSE CONTENT WITH RESONANCE. A TERM BORROWED FROM MUSIC, RESONANCE MEANS REVERBERATION OR ECHO, A SUBTLE QUALITY OF TONE OR TIMBRE... GRAPHIC DESIGNERS BRING A RESONANCE TO VISUAL COMMUNICATIONS THROUGH, FOR EXAMPLE, THE USE OF SCALE AND CONTRAST, CROPPING OF IMAGES, AND CHOICE OF TYPEFACES AND COLORS."

One of the most underrated ways of dealing with complex, repetitive messages within limited space is the use of iconic or diagrammatic substitution. This enables information to be put across in a more space-efficient, simplified manner that is easy for the reader to take in and retain. Information that otherwise would require a great deal of descriptive, convoluted text can be transposed by representative marks, shapes, annotations, or patterns. This presents the opportunity for more exciting use of color and composition than would be offered by a full written alternative. The signs and symbols designed for the Hong Kong KCR are excellent examples of conveying quite complex messages to a multilingual, multicultural audience.

Pictograms not only have a special role to play in communicating quite complex messages in a very space-efficient manner, but they also enable information to be available to everyone, whatever language they speak and whether or not they can read. If any one of these signs were to be replaced solely by words, the text would take up more space, especially in a number of different languages, and, more significantly, it is very unlikely that it would be understood as clearly.

Cultural systems forming recognizable visual registers such as letters, recipes, "news and views" pages, and financial information can, of course, be used literally but can more imaginatively be referenced to imply such contexts. If we look at Kym Abrams's design for The Joyce Foundation "Welfare to Work" report, the entire concept mimics a school notebook. Given the amount of technical and dry information to be included, this style provides interesting opportunities for dividing text as well as giving the reader a familiar and inviting environment.

The Joyce Foundation "Welfare to Work" report by Kym Abrams Design was a real challenge. "WE NEEDED TO PRESENT IT IN A QUICK, EASY-TO-UNDERSTAND MANNER," says Karen Gibson. "THE INFORMATION WAS VERY DRY AND A DESIGN APPROACH THAT WOULD LIVEN IT UP WAS CALLED FOR," she continues. "BY CREATING A NOTEBOOKLIKE DESIGN, WE WERE ABLE TO PRESENT THE MATERIAL IN SHORT 'LESSONS,' WHILE DESIGN ELEMENTS LIKE HIGHLIGHTING AND HANDWRITTEN NOTES IN THE MARGINS BROUGHT THE TEXT TO LIFE."

Earlier we discussed some of the advantages that technology provides. When handling complex layouts with lots of text and imagery, technology is often a blessing. The opportunities to layer information, to make elements opaque or transparent, the ability to cut out, to shape, to clone, etc., enable designers to play with hierarchies and compositions that would have been impossible just a short while ago.

So let's return to the original question: Do designers dread dealing with large quantities of information within limited spaces? There is no doubt that in some cases the answer is yes. But for the most part, the chance to deal with long or complex messages is a challenge from which most of us gain tremendous satisfaction—and judging by the examples we've received, a situation that often results in inspiring and effective design.

DESIGN FIRM **KYM ABRAMS DESIGN** ●
ART DIRECTION **KYM ABRAMS** ●
DESIGN **KAREN GIBSON** ●
PHOTOGRAPHY **MIKE WALKER** ●
CLIENT **THE JOYCE FOUNDATION** ●
PROJECT NAME **"WELFARE TO WORK"
SYNTHESIS REPORT**

DESIGN FIRM **WILSON HARVEY** ●
DESIGN **PAUL BURGESS** ● COPY
CHRIS WILSON, PAUL HENERDINE ●
CLIENT **WILSON HARVEY** ● PROJECT
NAME **PORTFOLIO**

Brochures produced to display design portfolios are notoriously tricky. Making the
selection of work to be included and deciding how much detail is to be given and how everything
should be laid out is very important.

"THE LARGE AMOUNTS OF INFORMATION ON THE INSIDE SPREADS ARE TREATED
WITH A DELICATE HAND TO ENSURE CLEAR HIERARCHY AND STRUCTURE," says Paul
Burgess of Wilson Harvey. Significant varieties in texture and tone, created through changes in
type sizes, weight, and spacing, together with background tints and photography, break up the
information and make it pleasing to view. Repetitions of a black arrow on a yellow box, fine gray
lines, and large typographic brackets act as visual glue. Despite the inclusion of considerable
information, predominantly landscape pages are skillfully engineered to avoid crowded
compositions.

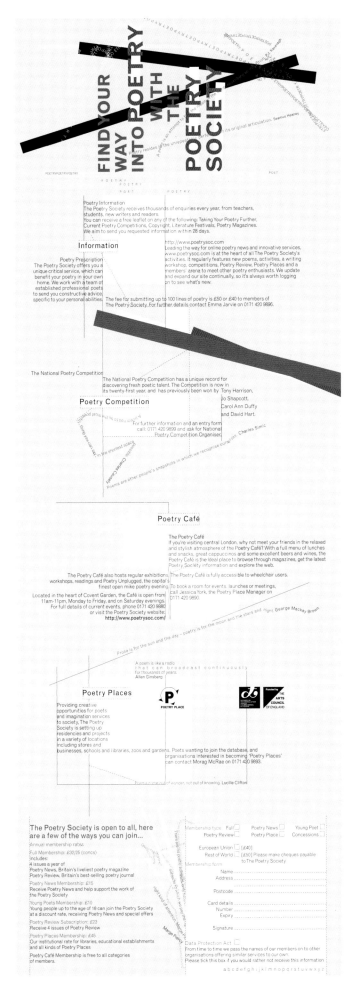

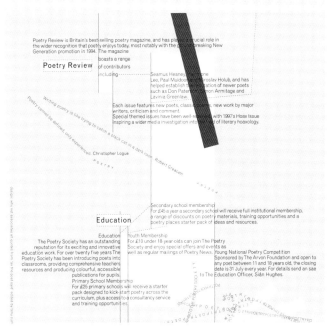

DESIGN FIRM **WHY NOT ASSOCIATES**
● PHOTOGRAPHY **PHOTODISC, ROCCO REDONDO** ● CLIENT **THE POETRY SOCIETY** ● PROJECT NAME **THE POETRY SOCIETY LEAFLET**

As with many projects that include a lot of rather dry informative text, The Poetry Society leaflet needed to be organized and presented in such a way as to coax and intrigue the casual reader into progressing beyond the first paragraph.

"THE TEXT WAS BROKEN DOWN," says David Ellis of Why Not Associates, "IN WAYS AIMED AT HIGHLIGHTING VARIOUS ISSUES, WHICH WERE INTERLACED WITH INSPIRATIONAL QUOTATIONS FROM WRITERS AND POETS, TO HELP THE LEAFLET BECOME MORE THAN JUST PURE INFORMATION." Although the designer chose to use a mix of orientations, measurements, alignments, and groupings, this leaflet successfully embodies the principle of continuance that we examined in the introduction to this section. The reader is led through different visual rhythms in a consistent direction managed by rules, flowing lines of type, and a subtle relationship with the center of each page.

The SmartTouch site is an extremely clever combination of informative detail and interactive game. "WE WANTED TO MAKE LEARNING FUN BY CREATING A GAME THAT CAN BE PLAYED ON- OR OFFLINE USING SMARTTOUCH USAGE SCENARIOS THAT PLAYERS CAN RELATE TO IN REAL LIFE," says Ivy Wong. The site is based on the format of a board game, with appealing animated illustrations and arrows to be counted around the perimeter of each window at the 'click' of a die. Whichever image a player 'lands on' has a story to tell about a specific circumstance when SmartTouch can help. There are clearly many instances where SmartTouch systems could make life easier (organizing a party from across the country or arranging personalized, confidential mailboxes). The game enables the player to experience these systems and identify with them in an enjoyable and comprehensive way. Overall, a huge amount of information and atmosphere is captured in this site, which would be very difficult to navigate and take in if it were presented in a more traditional text-and-image format.

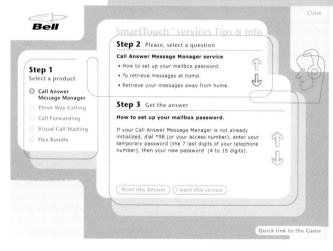

DESIGN FIRM **SPLASH INTERACTIVE/COSSETTE INTERACTIVE** ● ART DIRECTION **IVY WONG (SPLASH INTERACTIVE)** ● DESIGN **IVY WONG (SPLASH INTERACTIVE), MICHAEL CONVERY (COSSETTE INTERACTIVE), JONATHAN WEBBER (COSSETTE INTERACTIVE)** ● COPY **MICHAEL CONVERY (COSSETTE INTERACTIVE), JONATHAN WEBBER (COSSETTE INTERACTIVE)** ● ILLUSTRATION **IVY WONG, CSA** ● PHOTOGRAPHY **COSSETTE AND STOCK** ● CLIENT **BELL CANADA** ● PROJECT NAME **SMARTTOUCH SERVICES WEB SITE**

DESIGN FIRM **SAGMEISTER, INC.** ●
ART DIRECTION **STEFAN SAGMEISTER**
● DESIGN **HJALTI KARRISSON** ●
COPY **KAREN SALMANSOHN** ●
CLIENT **BLUE Q** ● PROJECT NAME
UNAVAILABLE SOAP

When a new line of soap becomes an entire philosophy, a tremendous amount of information has to be conveyed on its packaging—and a bar of soap is not exactly a large item! The exterior of the Unavailable package from Sagmeister, Inc. contains merely basic black-on-white product details. Open up the flap, and the entire interior surface is covered with Karen Salmonsohn's "15 proven principles for luring a nice man. . . or that sexier, more dangerous kind you really want!" By breaking the traditional expectations of packaging and using the inside as well as the outside, not only can the information be satisfactorily included, but it also becomes a metaphor for the product philosophy. The inaccessibility from the outside is available on the inside. To enforce this even more, says Stefan, "THE DEBOSSING OF 'UN' IN 'UNAVAILABLE' IS LESS DEEP THAN THE REST OF THE LOGOTYPE, AND AS YOU START USING THE SOAP, YOU GRADUALLY BECOME AVAILABLE!"

the pyramid a
the Louvre translate
as a triangle, or the Minist
of Pop Music as four dots
[and, typographically,
as two colons]

**"ECSTACITY WEAVES DIVERSE FRAGMENTS FROM SEVEN CITIES
AROUND THE WORLD INTO ONE MULTIFACETED URBAN FABRIC," says
David Ellis of Why Not Associates.** "THE AIM WAS TO LOAD UP THE DESIGN
WITH SPATIALITY. WE PLAYED WITH THE IMPLICATIONS OF ADJACENT IMAGES,
PUTTING ONE IMAGE INSIDE ANOTHER, BLURRING THEM AS IF THEY ARE
EXPERIENCED IN THE SAME MOMENT, AND ULTIMATELY WE ATTEMPTED TO CHARGE
UP TEXT, IMAGE, AND PAGE."

In many respects, the abundance of imagery and text was self-imposed in order to create an
environment that is as vital and open to interpretation as the imaginary city itself, but, Ellis
continues, "WE DECIDED AT AN EARLY STAGE TO KEEP THE MAIN TEXTS QUITE
SEPARATE FROM THE IMAGE COMPOSITIONS, SO YOU HAVE ALMOST TWO BOOKS IN
ONE, RUNNING ALONGSIDE EACH OTHER. ONLY PULL QUOTES, SHORT STORIES, AND
THE Z-TO-A HYPERGLOSSARY (WHICH RUNS BACKWARDS) WERE ALLOWED TO
INTERACT WITH IMAGES AND ADD OR AFFECT THEIR MEANING. IT WAS IMPORTANT
TO IMPOSE THIS ORDER TO PREVENT THE WHOLE BOOK FROM BECOMING TOO CHAOTIC
AND UNREADABLE."

This selection of double-page spreads demonstrates both visual and verbal excitement through
lively interplay of text and images. Every page is a surprise. The reader has little idea of what is
in store in the sections to come. Exciting mixes of scale, color, orientation, grouping, and textural
and tonal variety occur throughout. A huge amount of information is brought together with a
sensitive awareness of consistency as well as tremendous diversity. With so much happening, the
interplay of content creates fresh meaning at every glance. One of the most significant anchors
for cohesion is the presence of six ribbon page markers, representing and maintaining the
predominant color theme throughout.

DESIGN FIRM **WHY NOT ASSOCIATES**
● AUTHOR **NIGEL COATES** ●
PHOTOGRAPHY **VARIOUS** ● CLIENT
BOOTH-CLIBBORN EDITIONS ●
PROJECT NAME **GUIDE TO ECSTACITY**

DESIGN FIRM **DWELL** ● ART DIRECTION
JEANETTE ABBINK ● DESIGN **SHAWN
HAZEN** ● ILLUSTRATION **VARIOUS** ●
PHOTOGRAPHY **VARIOUS** ● CLIENT
DWELL **MAGAZINE** ● PROJECT NAME
DWELL

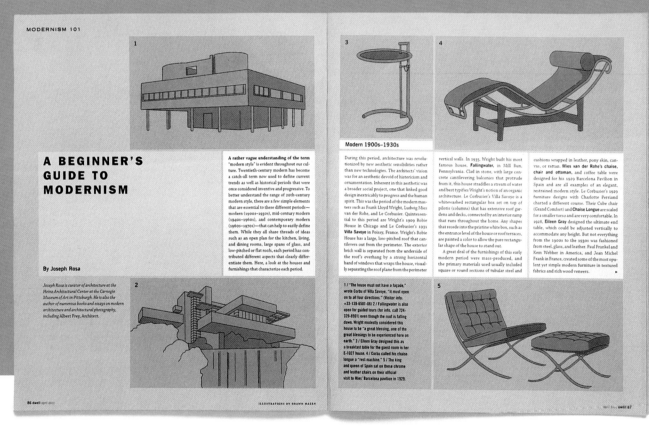

Dwell magazine offers commentary on modernist design and architecture and the impact it has on the real world. Typically, it has to cover a fair amount of copy, but needs to present it in a stylish way to reflect the subject matter. Throughout this issue, a strong grid structure holds the layouts together, and changes in pace and rhythm are achieved by different balances between text and image. "A Beginner's Guide to Modernism" combines examples of appropriately chosen illustration with well-written and visually organized copy, giving a comprehensive spread without crowding.

"Sing to me, show me, tell me," are the exclamations that emanate from Riorden's annual report for Corus Entertainment. "A HORIZONTAL FORMAT ALLOWED FOR BETTER INFORMATION MANAGEMENT," says Greer Hutchison, "GIVING MORE WHITE SPACE FOR IMAGERY AND LEAD IN CAPTIONS." An economic slowdown dictated budgetary constraints, and this report was reduced from 117 to 50 pages, making it a real challenge to present an exciting and diverse company in a more condensed style. Clever adaptation of full color within the front cover lifts and disguises the purely two-color interior. Changes within column widths, variations in typeface, and role reversals in orange and blue all aid visual interest.

DESIGN FIRM **THE RIORDON GROUP, INC.** ● ART DIRECTION **RICK RIORDEN** ● DESIGN **ALAN KRPAN** ● CLIENT **CORUS ENTERTAINMENT** ● PROJECT NAME *CORUS ANNUAL REPORT 2001*

DESIGN FIRM **WILSON HARVEY** ● ART DIRECTION
PAUL BURGESS ● PHOTOGRAPHY **KEV DUTTON** ●
CLIENT **SMITHKLINE BEECHAM** ● PROJECT NAME
PAIN EXPLAINED

Pain Explained is a 5.83" × 8.26" (14.5 cm × 21 cm) booklet packed with information about pain and how to manage it. Sections are differentiated through changes in type and background, and photography not only frees up breathing space but also makes subject changes obvious. The small format, particularly when it is full of information, can frequently suggest a rather unsophisticated or throwaway publication. Wilson Harvey skillfully overcame this through a well-considered layout, sensitive use of a fifth color—silver—and quality printing on weighty matte art stock.

BEATING STRESS
The moment you start to experience pain, your body isn't coping. So don't battle on. Stop working and take action to fight the pain. You'll probably have your own ways of coping, but consider trying some new relaxation ideas, such as the ones suggested here.
● Put a little time aside each day to relax: becoming a more relaxed person should help prevent future headaches.
● Ask for support. Delegate what tasks you can to others.
● Anticipate your next attack. Keep a diary of your headaches, and try to pinpoint the events, situations (and sometimes the people!) that trigger them.

DANGER SIGNS
ALTHOUGH HEADACHES ARE NEARLY ALWAYS UNPLEASANT, MOST CAN BE TREATED EASILY. VERY RARELY THERE MAY BE A MORE SERIOUS CAUSE. SO CONSULT YOUR DOCTOR IF:
● THE HEADACHE FOLLOWS AN INJURY
● THE HEADACHE REMAINS LONGER THAN SEVEN DAYS
● THE HEADACHE CHANGES IN CHARACTER FROM PREVIOUS HEADACHES
● YOU SUFFER FROM HEADACHES EVERY DAY – DO NOT CONTINUE TO TAKE PAINKILLERS
● YOU FEEL EXCESSIVELY DROWSY
● YOU HAVE BLURRED VISION
● YOU EXPERIENCE BALANCE PROBLEMS
● YOUR SPEECH BECOMES SLURRED
● YOU SUFFER ANY SORT OF FIT

IF YOU ARE AT ALL WORRIED BY YOUR HEADACHES, DON'T BE AFRAID TO ASK YOUR GP OR PHARMACIST FOR HELP.

HEADACHE

IT'S BEEN ESTIMATED THAT SIX IN EVERY TEN HEADACHES ARE CAUSED BY STRESS OR PRESSURE AT WORK.

HELP YOURSELF
If you suffer from frequent headaches, these measures should help:
● Don't miss a meal, as low blood sugar levels can bring on a headache.
● Chew some ginger, either raw or crystallised, at the first sign of a headache coming on.
● To help you relax, try an aromatherapy bath (lavender oil is good for headaches) or listening to restful music for quarter of an hour every evening. (But if you're pregnant, check with a doctor before using essential oils.)

ARE YOU STRESSED OUT?
Below are some of the signs of a stressed person. Ticking more than two boxes in either section means you should look carefully at that area of your life for ways of reducing stress.

SIGNS YOU MAY BE STRESSED AT WORK
Have you noticed an increase in:
☐ The amount of hours you work
☐ Failure to meet deadlines
☐ Fear at thought of going to work
☐ A sense of not being appreciated
☐ Inability to delegate

SIGNS YOU MAY BE STRESSED AT HOME
Have you noticed an increase in:
☐ Feeling unappreciated
☐ Snapping at partner or children
☐ A sense that nothing is being completed or done well
☐ Feeling isolated and/or feeling a lack of privacy
☐ Lethargy and exhaustion

YOU'LL PROBABLY KNOW THAT PEOPLE WHO DO A LOT OF WORK ON A COMPUTER ARE RECOMMENDED TO TAKE A TEN MINUTE BREAK EVERY HOUR TO REDUCE THE CHANCE OF TENSION HEADACHES. BUT DO YOU KNOW YOU SHOULD ALSO DO THIS WHEN PLAYING COMPUTER GAMES OR WATCHING TV?

2 PAIN EXPLAINED

IT SEEMS THAT THE PARTICULARLY PAINFUL TYPE OF HEADACHE KNOWN AS MIGRAINE HAS ALWAYS BEEN WITH US. THE FIRST RECORDED MIGRAINE IS DEPICTED IN A PAPYRUS SCROLL DATING FROM BEFORE THE BIRTH OF CHRIST.

Why some people get it and others don't is still not known, although there is probably a genetic component. Pain is our body's signal to the brain that something is wrong, and it would seem that people who suffer from migraines inherit a particularly sensitive mechanism for detecting potential 'danger signals'. While the rest of us might see tension, missed meals or changes of temperature as something uncomfortable, a migraine sufferer registers these, and other, migraine triggers as being potentially very dangerous, and therefore very painful, at a much earlier stage than would be expected. It is also possible that female hormones – which men have, too, although in small amounts – affect the onset of migraine. Although it's still not completely understood, the fact that women are more affected points to a hormonal link. It would also explain why women are more likely to get a migraine attack on the first day of menstruation.

PAIN EXPLAINED
DURING THE PRE-MIGRAINE STAGE (STAGE ONE) WHILE UNDER STRESS, BUT BEFORE PAIN ACTUALLY STARTS, STRESS HORMONES THAT AFFECT THE BLOOD VESSELS ARE RELEASED. THESE CAUSE BLOOD VESSELS AROUND THE BRAIN TO CONSTRICT. IN RESPONSE, THE BODY RELEASES HORMONES TO MAKE THE BLOOD VESSELS RELAX AND DILATE (STAGE TWO). WHILE THE BODY IS TENSE, IT'S AN UPHILL JOB FOR THE HORMONES TO WORK, BUT WHEN THE PERSON RELAXES, AFTER THE STRESS IS OVER, THE EFFECT OF THE RELAXING HORMONES IS MUCH STRONGER, THE BLOOD VESSELS OVER-RELAX, OR, RATE TOO MUCH (STAGE THREE) AND THE RESULT IS SEVERE PAIN.

IT'S OFTEN ASSUMED THAT MIGRAINES ARE SIMPLY HEADACHES. BUT A MIGRAINE IS QUITE DIFFERENT. IT'S A 'VASCULAR' HEADACHE (ITS ORIGINS ARE IN CHANGES IN THE BLOOD VESSELS) RATHER THAN A 'TENSION' HEADACHE (WHICH ARISES BECAUSE OF MUSCULAR CONSTRICTION). HOWEVER, JUST AS WITH TENSION HEADACHES, RELAX-ING CAN ALSO HELP A MIGRAINE. BY RECOGNISING STAGE ONE, THE PRE-MIGRAINE STAGE, AND TAKING STEPS TO RELAX THEN, BEFORE THE STRESS HORMONES ARE RELEASED, THE MIGRAINE MAY NEVER GET A CHANCE TO TAKE HOLD.

MIGRAINE

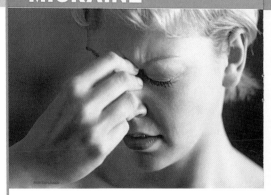

HELP YOURSELF
● If you feel a migraine is about to take hold, these measures should help. As soon as you suspect the onset of migraine, take your usual medication and rest. Preferably, sleep. There is clear evidence that sleep plus medication is far more effective than medication alone.
● Have a sweet, fizzy drink. Sweetness raises blood sugar levels and low blood sugar levels, prior to an attack, have been shown to be a common trigger for migraine in many sufferers.
● Learn the symptoms that precede your migraines. This will help you anticipate and treat a migraine before it takes hold. It's also common to feel tired and lethargic, or conversely, exuberant and 'high'. So keeping a diary will help you understand your pattern.

MORE HELP?
MIGRAINE ACTION ASSOCIATION
01932 352468

CITY MIGRAINE CLINIC
0171 251 3322

MIGRAINE TRUST
0171 831 4818

PAIN EXPLAINED

DESIGN FIRM **THE RIORDON DESIGN GROUP, INC.** ● ART DIRECTION **RIC RIORDON** ● DESIGN **AMY MONTGOMERY** ● PHOTOGRAPHY **GRIMES PHOTOGRAPHY** ● CLIENT **MINI-YO-WE CAMP** ● PROJECT NAME **MINI-YO-WE BROCHURE**

When a client requests that thousands of names be included on a small brochure, it's easy to have a distinct sinking feeling! The Riordon Design Group, however, used this directive to create a lively response for the Mini-Yo-We publicity material. The action-filled images, bright colors, metallic ink, and "funky fonts" on one side of a folded accordion style format are inviting to young people. Names reversed through silver in an all-over row-upon-row pattern fulfill the client's request on the reverse, making a striking contrast. A silver 1.5" (4 cm) deep sleeve holds the closed piece in place as a final touch.

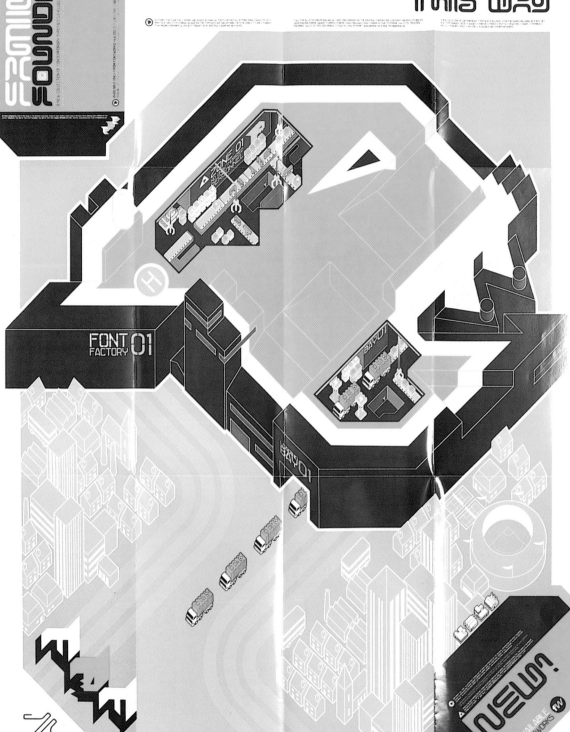

DESIGN FIRM **IDENTIKAL** ● DESIGN
NICK HAYES, ADAM HAYES ● CLIENT
FONTWORKS ● PROJECT NAME
FONTWORKS POSTER

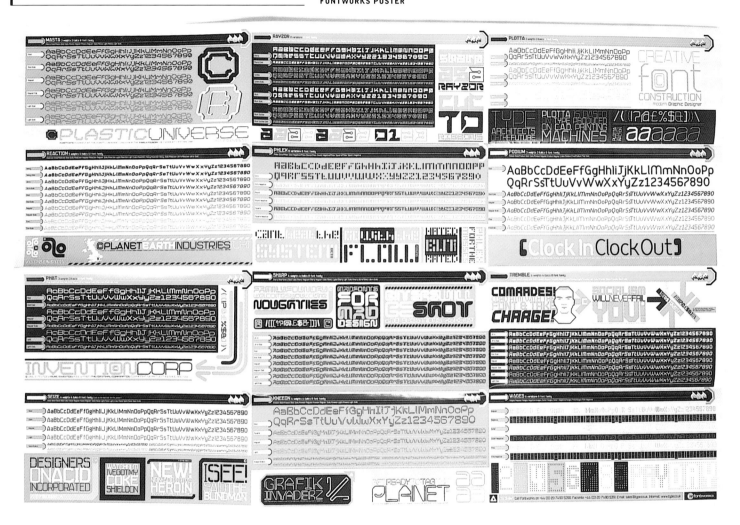

The brief for this Fontworks poster was to show the complete families of twelve different typefaces and to effectively demonstrate them in use. The Hayes twins of Identikal also consider it their duty to keep their own personal style recognizable throughout, making the space, despite being 33" × 23.5" (84 cm × 59.4 cm), very precious. The poster folds into twelve sections, which on one side provide equal areas for each typeface, and on the other, a humorous platform for the "font factory." A full and vibrant two-color montage of letterforms, symbols, graphic bars, and shapes captures the type styles, while a wacky illustration confirms that the use of these typefaces in designs is intended for contemporary youth culture.

DESIGN FIRM **PAPRIKA** ● ART
DIRECTION **LOUIS GAGNON** ● DESIGN
FRANÇOIS LECLERC ● PHOTOGRAPHY
MICHEL TOUCHETTE ● CLIENT
BELAIR DIRECT ● PROJECT NAME
EN DIRECT NEWSLETTER

This Belair newsletter, the final issue of a ten-year-old publication, is expected to represent the disparate events from some forty issues, most predating desktop publishing.

Inspiration has clearly come from various collecting environments, such as the bulletin board, the scrapbook, and the souvenir album. According to François Leclerc, "THE INITIAL STAGES FOR EACH SPREAD ACTUALLY INVOLVED THE TACTILE PROCESSES OF CUTTING, TEARING, ASSEMBLING, ARRANGING, AND PASTING, ADDING OFFICE ITEMS SUCH AS SCISSORS, PAPER CLIPS, AND HOLE PUNCHES TO LIVEN UP THE OVERALL EFFECT." The challenge was not only to overcome the reproduction problems of mainly hard copy archive material but also to provide a distinctive visual cohesion and coherence. Although each element was carefully organized, the juxtaposing and overlaying give the impression of a casual and unplanned composition that is expected in this environment.

EnDirect, suite et fin !

Depuis le premier numéro publié en juin 1982, En Direct a été le témoin de notre vie professionnelle. Vingt ans plus tard, BELAIR*direct* a le vent dans les voiles et, pour en témoigner, En Direct se joindra au nouveau bulletin interne d'ING Québec pour refléter notre réalité régionale et notre appartenance au Groupe ING. Ce n'est pas une fin, mais une renaissance. ¶ Plutôt que de filer à l'anglaise, nous avons pensé faire un survol des vingt ans que nous avons vécus ensemble, voir le chemin parcouru, nous revoir tels que nous étions, et du coup, se faire plaisir ! Ce numéro d'archives se veut plus un répertoire des bons coups et des faits saillants qu'un historique détaillé, une sorte de témoignage de nos coups de cœur. ¶ En vingt ans, nous avons souligné le départ de deux présidents, salué l'arrivée d'un troisième et vu le retour du deuxième ; aperçu notre collaborateur Louis Cyr en Rabi Jacob, spéculé sur l'allocation de la piastre à Denis, survécu à la tempête de verglas et au bogue de l'an 2000, connu deux transformations de notre marque, pique-niqué sur l'herbe, puis sous le chapiteau, accumulé des prix, formé des partenariats, pris le virage Internet, lancé la *Police qui pardonne*, inauguré un nouveau siège social et fait la fête, souvent ! En Direct a souhaité la bienvenue aux employés de la Métropolitaine générale et appris à parler anglais pour accueillir ceux de la Constitution. ¶ Aujourd'hui, nous disons au revoir à nos collègues de l'Ontario et un gros merci à Kathleen Martin, notre complice de la première heure à Toronto. L'*Insider*, le bulletin de la région Centre/Atlantique prendra la relève et nous souhaitons la bienvenue à son éditrice, Diana Dumencic. Au Québec, l'équipe de rédaction, notre columnist, David Lazar, et nos collaborateurs en région, feront tandem avec nos collègues d'ING pour produire le nouveau journal. Plus on est de fous… ¶ Je tiens à VOUS remercier d'avoir fait d'En Direct le bulletin interne le plus apprécié de ses lecteurs — on ne voulait surtout pas se priver de le dire une dernière fois ! ¶ En Direct n'est pas mort ; vive la nouvelle publication régionale ! — LOUISE FOURNIER, ÉDITRICE

As a reissue of an existing LP, the CD design for *Boss Tenors in Orbit!* is expected to capture recognizable styling. It is also intended to attract a new audience, with both fresh visual input and a great deal of background information. The CD case and enclosed leaflet use rich combinations of bold and lightweight type to express musical rhythms that are perpetuated throughout. These, together with contrasting black-and-white images, complement and carry the text-heavy sections.

DESIGN FIRM **MOTOKO HADA** ● ART
DIRECTION **HOLLIS KING** ● DESIGN
MOTOKO HADA ● PHOTOGRAPHY
TED WILLIAMS, MOTOKO HADA ●
CLIENT **THE VERVE MUSIC GROUP** ●
PROJECT NAME ***BOSS TENORS
IN ORBIT!***

DESIGN FIRM **IDAHO** ● ART DIRECTION
MARK LAYCOCK ● DESIGN **MARK**
LAYCOCK ● ILLUSTRATION **WARREN**
MACENZIE ● CLIENT
CULTURESHOCK ● PROJECT NAME
CULTURESHOCK WEB SITE,
WWW.CULTURESHOCK2002.COM

Cultureshock has been the largest happening of its kind to be held in England's northwest. Complementing the 2002 Commonwealth Games, it encompasses a wide program of arts, cultural events, and exhibitions. This Web site has been an ideal way to provide a worldwide audience with a huge amount of complex material. A week-by-week calendar, news, and other sections full of information are easily accessed. Viewers are able to pursue their area of specific interest quickly by using the comprehensive menus and abundant links. Beautiful photography provides colorful support to Idaho's distinctive background tones, which help to distinguish between varying subjects.

DESIGN FIRM **ROUNDEL** ● ART
DIRECTION **MICHAEL DENNY** ●
DESIGN **STEVE PARKER** ● CLIENT
KOWLOON-CANTON RAILWAY ●
PROJECT NAME **KCR LIGHT RAIL MAP**

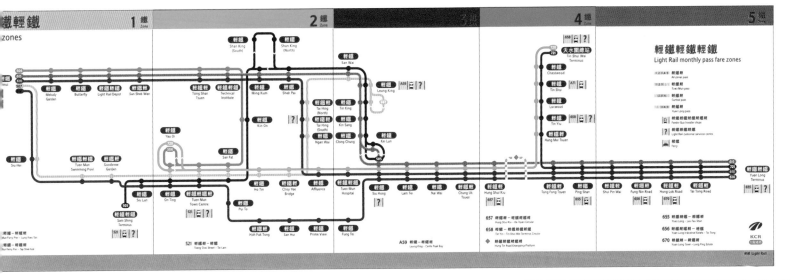

The Kowloon-Canton Railway map has to convey a great deal in a manner that is easy to understand and is technically correct. "THE MAP HAS TO CLEARLY SHOW THE FARE ZONES, EACH STATION BY NAME (IN ENGLISH AND CHINESE), PLUS ALL THE INDIVIDUAL ROUTES," says Charlie Kemp, project manager for Roundel. Geographical accuracy is sacrificed, with simple yet coherent diagrammatic systems representing the information. "CAREFUL LAYOUT AND USE OF COLOR ARE THE KEY TO MAKING THE MAP EASY TO READ, BUT EVEN IN BLACK AND WHITE AND REDUCED TO A SMALL SCALE FOR PRINTED TIMETABLES, ALL THE INFORMATION IS STILL CLEAR," Kemp concludes.

DESIGN FIRM **MATT AND GEORGE** ●
DESIGN **JACK SCHULZE, MATT HYDE,**
GEORGE AGNELLI ● COPY **PHIL**
BAINES, CATHERINE DIXON ●
PHOTOGRAPHY **PHIL BAINES, JACK**
SCHULZE, MATT HYDE, TIMO ARNALL ●
CLIENT **MATT AND GEORGE** ● PROJECT
NAME **PUBLIC LETTERING WEB SITE,**
WWW.PUBLICLETTERING.COM

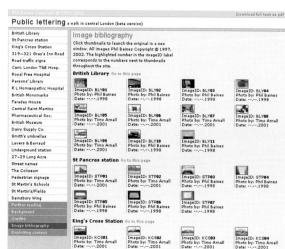

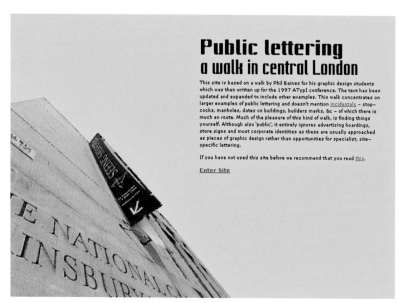

Public lettering
a walk in central London

This site is based on a walk by Phil Baines for his graphic design students which was then written up for the 1997 ATypI conference. The text has been updated and expanded to include other examples. This walk concentrates on larger examples of public lettering and doesn't mention incidentals – stop-cocks, manholes, dates on buildings, builders marks, &c – of which there is much en route. Much of the pleasure of this kind of walk, is finding things yourself. Although also 'public', it entirely ignores advertising hoardings, store signs and most corporate identities as these are usually approached as pieces of graphic design rather than opportunities for specialist, site-specific lettering.

If you have not used this site before we recommend that you read this.

Enter Site

This fascinating online interpretation of Phil Baines's public lettering walk, which he originally devised for his students, enables viewers to take a virtual tour of central London and zoom in to illustrative examples of lettering visible from the streets. There is a great deal of information that needs to be included in the site. George Agnelli explains how he dealt with some of the challenges of this project. "IT WAS INEVITABLE THAT SOME USERS WOULD HAVE TO SCROLL THE PAGE TO VIEW CERTAIN CONTENT, SO A DECISION WAS MADE TO ADOPT THE 'DESIGN ABOVE THE FOLD' PHILOSOPHY IN ORDER TO MAKE THE VISIBLE PORTION OF THE PAGE AS INTERESTING AS POSSIBLE. TO MAXIMIZE THE AMOUNT OF INFORMATION WE COULD FIT INTO THE SPACE AVAILABLE, WE USED DHTML TO ENABLE US TO BUILD PARTS OF THE PAGE THAT COULD CHANGE AT THE CLICK OF A LINK. EXAMPLES OF THIS CAN BE FOUND IN THE 'DETAILS' BOXES AND ALSO IN THE FOOTNOTES IN THE MAIN TEXT. CLICKING THE 'NOTE' LINK EXPANDS THE TEXT TO SHOW THE FOOTNOTE. THIS MEANS THE USER IS ABLE TO VIEW ALL THE INFORMATION ABOUT A PIECE OF PUBLIC LETTERING WITHOUT HAVING TO JUMP TO A NEW PAGE."

This site demonstrates the online advantages of handling large amounts of information within limited space by promoting the viewing of different areas at different times and in different combinations.

DESIGN FIRM **TEIKNA DESIGN, INC.** ●
DESIGN **CLAUDIA NERI** ● COPY **CLAUDIA
NERI** ● ILLUSTRATION **CLAUDIA NERI** ●
PHOTOGRAPHY **CLAUDIA NERI** ● CLIENT
SELF-PROMOTION ● PROJECT NAME
GREEK INTERLUDE

**Finding refreshment in "going back to basics" and
working with her hands instead of a
keyboard,** Claudia Neri has produced Greek Interlude
using collages of found and collected detritus, combined
with free-flowing, hand-lettered text. Copy runs through
and around imagery, creating not only meaningful tales but
also textural backgrounds and shapes, roughly cut-out
photographs, as well as tickets and maps. And after dealing
with all this information, Neri still had the energy to hand
stitch the binding!

"THE FRONT AND BACK COVERS OF
WHERE LOCALS HIKE," says
Matthew Clark,
**"ACCOMMODATE A LARGE
VOLUME OF TEXT AND
STORYTELLING IN AN
ATTEMPT TO ELEVATE THE
PERCEPTION OF THE BOOK
AND INTRIGUE THE
READER."**

Clark chose to take advantage of the
quantity of information and filled the
space with a lively synergy of type and
imagery. Handwritten text appears
scratched through the surface of
landscape photography and is grouped
and orientated in a casual manner, as
if unplanned. Differing sizes and
weights partially determine
sequencing, but above all, a sense of
inquisitiveness prevails. The viewer
cannot resist the temptation to read
every little cameo of writing, which
must, it seems, tell of personal and
somewhat private experiences!

DESIGN FIRM **HÉPA! DESIGNS** ●
DESIGN **MATTHEW CLARK** ● COPY
CRAIG COPELAND ● PHOTOGRAPHY
KATHY COPELAND ● ILLUSTRATION
MATTHEW CLARK ● CLIENT **VOICE IN
THE WILDERNESS PRESS** ● PROJECT
NAME *WHERE LOCALS HIKE*

DESIGN FIRM **GROUP BARONET** ● ART
DIRECTION **META NEWHOUSE** ●
DESIGN **BRONSON MA** ● CLIENT
TEXAS INTERNATIONAL THEATRICAL
ARTS SOCIETY ● PROJECT NAME
TITAS BROCHURE

Program listings and timetables tend to fall into a slightly unappealing category of projects for designers, as they inevitably have to include an abundance of dates, times, venues, and names, which can be extremely space consuming and repetitive, in a restricted format.

"I WAS DETERMINED TO GIVE THE READERS A RESTFUL OPENING SPACE IN THE BROCHURE TO COMPLEMENT THE MORE CONGESTED SECTIONS," says Bronson Ma. To do this, he created additional space with a flyleaf for each of the three entertainment genres. The introductions were then able to clearly and simply set the scene before opening up to all the necessary detail. Vertical and horizontal lines, type styles, photographs, and colors link the spreads, giving equal importance to imagery and text.

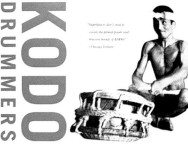

DESIGN FIRM **ORIGIN DESIGN** ●
DESIGN **ROBERT ACHTEN** ● CLIENT
ICEBREAKER ● PROJECT NAME
ICEBREAKER CATALOGUE

We featured one of the Icebreaker catalogs in the introduction, showing pages that involved little information in a comparatively generous space. This is only possible because of the clever way in which other pages are designed to communicate considerably more. Rachel Paine of Origin Design tells us of the challenge in presenting 125 products in various formats, with breakdowns of style, color, sex, and size all within a fifty-six page, 10.2" × 6.4" (26 cm × 17 cm) catalog. In one spread, nineteen photographs of seven products in varying colors are shown in an airy manner. Paine comments, "A BALANCE HAD TO BE REACHED TO SHOW IMAGES THAT CLEARLY DEPICTED THE CLOTHING (SO PEOPLE CAN MAKE A PURCHASE DECISION) AS WELL AS CAPTURING A DEGREE OF PERSONALITY AND BRAND ATTITUDE." To complement the full pages, introductions focus on a larger photograph that highlights more garment detailing. It is really interesting, however, to note the number of design systems, from color coding and type styling to positioning and surface treatment (matte or gloss) that quite subtly convey a lot of information. "WE HAD TO PROVIDE A GREAT LEVEL OF TECHNICAL SUPPORT THROUGH A BALANCE OF COPY AND GRAPHIC IMAGERY," Paine says. Uncoated stock differentiates between product descriptions and the more technical data concerning complicated fabric structures and tolerances. Diagrams, illustrations, tables, carefully selected photographs and editorial language are designed to maximize the space available.

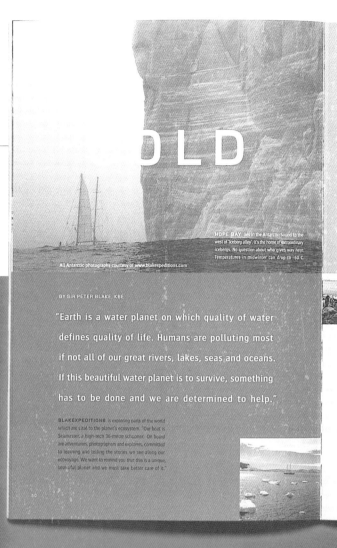

OLD

HOPE BAY lies in the Antarctic Sound to the west of 'iceberg alley'. It's the home of extraordinary icebergs. No question about who gives way here. Temperatures in midwinter can drop to -60°C.

All Antarctic photographs courtesy of www.blakexpeditions.com

BY SIR PETER BLAKE, KBE

"Earth is a water planet on which quality of water defines quality of life. Humans are polluting most if not all of our great rivers, lakes, seas and oceans. If this beautiful water planet is to survive, something has to be done and we are determined to help."

BLAKEXPEDITIONS is exploring parts of the world which are vital to the planet's ecosystem. "Our boat is Seamaster, a high-tech 36-metre schooner. On board are adventurers, photographers and explorers, committed to learning and telling the stories we see along our ecovoyage. We want to remind you that this is a unique, beautiful planet and we must take better care of it."

50

FROM SEAMASTER Sunday 14 January 2001, 10 miles north-west of Hope Bay at the entrance to Antarctic Sound at the top of the Antarctic Peninsula. Hope Bay is off to the west side of 'iceberg alley' – where many bergs broken off from the ice in the Weddell Sea come through Antarctic Sound on their journey out into the south Atlantic. All this afternoon, rows of bergs of different shapes and sizes have been lining both sides of our course as we head south. Many are grounded in shallow waters (if anyone can call 100 metre deep water shallow) and we are weaving our way between a great number of smaller bits. We have to have an iceberg watch on the bow at all times, looking out for the bits that are hard to see... To be here and see excess fresh water transformed into pieces of Antarctic ice shelf now floating past is to marvel at nature. To understand how everything affects everything else is a basic principle that we are all going to have to learn, believe and understand. If we can get the simple but vital messages out to the world about the need to make every aspect of our environment sustainable, then I will begin to feel that our expeditions over the next 5 years and beyond can make a difference. If we can convince millions of individuals that they need to change their attitudes, then we will have been successful. IT'S TIME, MAKE A DIFFERENCE. Best wishes from all on board Seamaster. Kind regards, Peter.

ANTARCTIC PENINSULA
WEDDELL SEA
SOUTH POLE

Sir Peter Blake and the entire crew of Seamaster are wearing icebreaker bodyfit under layer beneath icebreaker sport mid layer.

"The icebreaker garments are fantastic. THEY HAVE PERFORMED WAY BEYOND ANYONE'S EXPECTATIONS. I think there were those in the crew who might have thought I was extolling the virtues of icebreaker too much at the beginning of the trip but no longer. They are now all converts. I wear my icebreaker under my wet weather gear, under my dry suit when diving, round the boat, and to bed at night." SIR PETER BLAKE KBE

51

DEADVLEI is a bed of a river which dried up millions of years ago. Skeletons of trees 500 years old are preserved by the dry, hot atmosphere. The temperature ranges from 35°C during the day to 5°C at night.

BY NIGEL KNOWLES, LIVE FROM NAMIBIA

"The owners of Nywenya lodge, near the Kruger National Park, had just lost their dog to a twelve-foot long inhabitant of Crocodile River. As we took preventative measures against malaria with gin and tonic we contemplated our own position in the food chain. Don warned us to keep the windows tightly shut the next day as we viewed the lions...

...We headed north-west to Botswana where we shared a campsite with some hippopotamus. In Zimbabwe, Kim took shots of the majestic Victoria Falls as we shortened her camera from torrential mist. A military convoy escorted us through the Caprivi Strip, south of the Angolan border. Hosts of spectacular scenery lasted into days as we headed south through the deserts, half buried ghost towns and restricted diamond areas of Namibia. In was not expecting the road ahead to be under construction. The 4WD rolled 3 times as it slowed from 100km/hr. We pondered our luck as we retrieved camera and camping gear from the road. Luckily the only serious injury was to our reputation."

Nigel, Jo, Donald and Kim all chose icebreaker superfine. (Photos in circles by Donald Dale.)

"The climates of the countries in the south of Africa were diverse like its cultures and unpredictable like its wildlife. I found my icebreaker was purpose built for all the environments we visited. The garments layered comfortably for protection from the cold winds of the Atlantic Ocean, and a single item of clothing allowed air to pass through while hiking over desert sands to Deadvlei. The four of us each went to the countries in the south of Africa for different reasons. The reasons we all wear icebreaker are the same." NIGEL KNOWLES

DESIGN FIRM **PISCATELLO DESIGN CENTRE** ● DESIGN **ROCCO PISCATELLO** ● HISTORIAN **MAUREEN MURPHY** ● PHOTOGRAPHY **ROCCO PISCATELLO, REVEN T. C. NIRMAN** ● CLIENT **BATTERY PARK CITY AUTHORITY** ● PROJECT NAME **IRISH HUNGER MEMORIAL**

In the introduction to this section we recognized that the allocated space for an eligible piece doesn't need to be small—only that the available space is limited in comparison to the amount of information to be included. The Irish Hunger Memorial, located in Battery Park City, New York, stretches almost 2 miles (3.2 kilometers) around its base and gives structure and meaning to the story of the great Irish famine. As Rocco Piscatello explains, "WE HAD THE PROBLEM OF DEALING WITH AUTOBIOGRAPHIES, LETTERS, ORAL TRADITIONS, PARLIAMENTARY REPORTS, POEMS, RECIPES, SONGS, AND STATISTICS." In fact, because the memorial is intended to relate to the unfortunate ongoing famines across the world, the text also needs to be flexible, enabling easy changes and updating. "LIKE THE MEMORIAL'S ORGANIC LANDSCAPE," adds Piscatello, "THE TEXT, TOO, IS LIVING AND CONSTANTLY KEEPING PACE WITH THE WORLD AT LARGE." Just as ticker tape strips of messages bring news and greetings across distances, so Piscatello has evoked this medium to convey the mix of considerable informal and formal information.

DESIGN FIRM **THE INDEPENDENT ON SUNDAY** ● DESIGN **CAROLYN ROBERTS** ● PROJECT NAME **YOU'VE GOT THE LOOK**

If this page were not the size of a broadsheet newspaper, it could easily pass for part of a fashion magazine. Typical of newspaper articles, a great deal of copy is shown, but Carolyn Roberts has succeeded in achieving stylish synergy with different levels of text, image, and small amounts of carefully engineered space. Type runs around cut-out photographs; fine rules act as decoration and demarcation to the three areas of the article. Sensitive use of tinted text together with well-selected changes of weight and scale create interesting textural and tonal changes on this full page of enjoyable fashion comment.

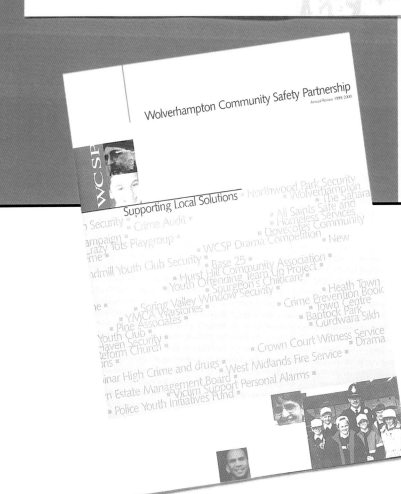

DESIGN FIRM **BRIGHT PINK** ● DESIGN
JESSICA GLASER, CAROLYN KNIGHT
● CLIENT **WCSP** ● PROJECT NAME
WCSP ANNUAL REVIEW

"WE CAN BE CERTAIN OF ONE THING," we exclaimed in
the introduction to this book, **"THERE WILL BE A LOT TO
SAY IN THIS REPORT, WITH SOME SECTIONS NEEDING TO
CONTAIN GREAT AMOUNTS OF INFORMATION WHILE
OTHERS THAT ARE NO LESS IMPORTANT SAY
CONSIDERABLY LESS."**

A limited color palette, contrast of scale, integrated typographic systems, and
spatial dynamics allow this report to present its comparatively dry information
in a visually interesting and surprising manner. Letter spacing, word spacing,
leading, and image relationships are bound together in a series of cumulative
associations. The arrangement of large, closely leaded type is reflected in
even larger butting-up letterforms and image boxes, while smaller widely
spaced lines are both complementary and essential to the inclusion of white
space on other pages. The resulting textural and tonal mélange communicates
on an abstract level that is not only interesting, but also inviting to read and
easy to comprehend.

Featuring two front covers and involving the surprising use of "erasing" thermochromic ink that disappears with the heat of the readers' hands, Fishten has produced this sixteen-page accordion-fold leaflet to promote the duel center exhibition, "Time and Distance Cannot Erase." One side of this publication features full-color photographs of the exhibits, and the other provides space for an extensive introduction, biographies, and artists' statements. The introduction is divided into four sections that run vertically down the center of pages, with statements and biographies sitting to the left and right of this division. Woodward and Hartmann have interestingly selected very pale ink, which has the effect of lightening the impact of the considerable volume of information.

DESIGN FIRM **FISHTEN** ● DESIGN
GILES WOODWARD, KELLY HARTMANN
● COPY **JOANNE MARION, KARL
LAVOY** ● CLIENT **MEDICINE HAT
MUSEUM AND ART GALLERY** ●
PROJECT NAME **TIME AND DISTANCE
CANNOT ERASE**

DESIGN FIRM **[I]E DESIGN** ● ART
DIRECTION **MARCIE CARSON** ● DESIGN
MARCIE CARSON, CYA NELSON ●
CLIENT **EL CAMINO RESOURCES** ●
PROJECT NAME *EL CAMINO
RESOURCES ANNUAL REPORT*

**Typically, the *El Camino Resources Annual Report* is required to include
a considerable amount of rather dry material,** which [i]e
design has chosen to interpret in a style that reflects the company's leading
role in new technologies. Layers of computer-generated imagery and columns
of text create a visual synthesis. Images blend into and behind text, and type
mechanically curves round shaped picture boxes. Interesting hierarchies and
changes of texture and tone are developed through typographic detailing, and
the viewer is tempted to enjoy the reading experience.

DESIGN FIRM **THE INDEPENDENT ON SUNDAY PRODUCTION** ● ART DIRECTION **CAROLYN ROBERTS** ● DESIGN **ADELE BREARLEY** ● CLIENT *THE INDEPENDENT ON SUNDAY* ● PROJECT NAME **SPORTS ACTIVE COVER**

Attention to detailing in this broadsheet newspaper cover is superb. Consequently, although the bulk of the text conforms to traditional formatting, the general impression of the layout is striking and stylish. Carefully considered typographic changes in size, weight, orientation, column width, and color coordinate throughout the headings, captions, and listings to break up the information. The mix of squared-up photographs, cut-out images, black-and-white shots, color shots, dynamic contrasts of scale, and changing angles bring the layout to life.

"ONE OF THE MOST CHALLENGING ASPECTS OF THIS PROJECT" says Peter Campbell of Infographics, **"IS THE MAINTAINING OF AN OVERALL CLEAN LOOK WHILE STILL ENGAGING READERS AND ENCOURAGING THEM TO TACKLE THE ENORMOUS AMOUNT OF TEXT."** Space is engineered in a number of calculated ways. A condensed font, at minimum size and leading for legibility, is used for all of the body text. Four narrow columns with margins that come right out to the edge of the page give room for an outside column for imagery and force the copy into accessible chunks. Headings are established through changes in weight and color rather than scale, and generally photographs are kept small, with only the addition of fine orange lines echoing the company symbol being allowed as a concession to decoration.

DESIGN FIRM **INFOGRAPHIC DESIGN**
● ART DIRECTION **LEANNE BARNETT, PETER CAMPBELL** ● DESIGN **LEANNE BARNETT** ● CLIENT **AUSTRALIAN PHOTONICS COOPERATIVE RESEARCH CENTRE** ● PROJECT NAME *AUSTRALIAN PHOTONICS COOPERATIVE RESEARCH CENTRE ANNUAL REPORT 2000*

DESIGN FIRM **KARACTERS DESIGN GROUP** ● ART DIRECTION **MATTHEW CLARK** ● CLIENT **CLEARLY CANADIAN BEVERAGE CORPORATION** ● PROJECT NAME **CLEARLY CANADIAN PACKAGING LABEL**

Clearly Canadian Water needs to distinguish itself from other water products, as it is enhanced with up to ten times the normal concentration of oxygen and is sold in innovative containers that help to prolong the oxygen's retention. As a consequence, instead of displaying minimal graphics, the labels have to be crammed with text, diagrams, and icons. Karacters Design Group has constructively used the situation to reference scientific/medical labeling. Each element of information is framed by a fine rule and butts up to the next in precise "jigsaw" fashion. "THE CHALLENGE WAS TO ORGANIZE A MODULAR GRID THAT COMMUNICATED THE BRAND FIRST, BENEFITS AND FORMULATION SECOND, AND LEGAL TEXT LAST," says Matthew Clark. Although colors have been selected for flavor coding, they are primary colors that perpetuate the required visual language.

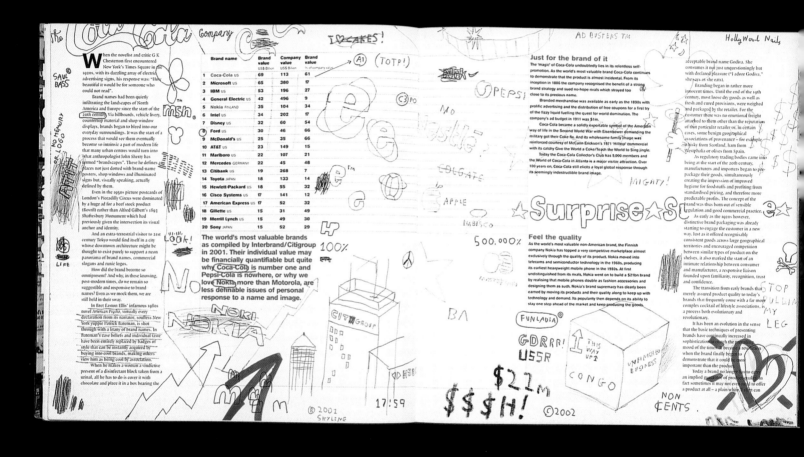

Although conventional typographic elements make up much of these layouts in *M-Real* magazine, they are considerably modified by hand-drawn scribbles and "thumbnails." Throughout the publication, marker pen and pencil embellishments add information and meaning. The spreads are packed with vitality, as if a conversation is taking place between the regular type and the hand-drawn sections, filling the pages with data that can add up to more than the sum of the individual parts, and readers may absorb as many or as few levels as they choose.

DESIGN FIRM **JOHN BROWN CITRUS**
PUBLISHING ● DESIGN **JEREMY**
LESLIE ● CLIENT **M-REAL**
MAGAZINE ● PROJECT NAME **M-REAL**,
"BRAND VALUE"

Group Baronet has produced this brochure for the Dallas Convention and Visitors' Bureau to promote the city as an exciting place to visit by day or night.

Attractions such as theaters, restaurants, shopping, sports, and music are presented in an exciting manner across the many faces of this broadsheet. Space is at a premium with so much to see and do. Group Baronet has successfully conveyed this hive of activity by filling every available space with multisized cut-out images, text that highlights many attractions, and on the reverse, a huge, illustrated map packed with a multitude of amusing representations of every conceivable activity within the area.

DESIGN FIRM **GROUP BARONET** •
ART DIRECTION **META NEWHOUSE** •
DESIGN **BRONSON MA** • COPY **MAX
WRIGHT** • ILLUSTRATION **JACK
UNRUH, VARIOUS** • CLIENT **DALLAS
CONVENTION AND VISITORS' BUREAU**
• PROJECT NAME **DALLAS BY
DAY/NIGHT BROCHURE**

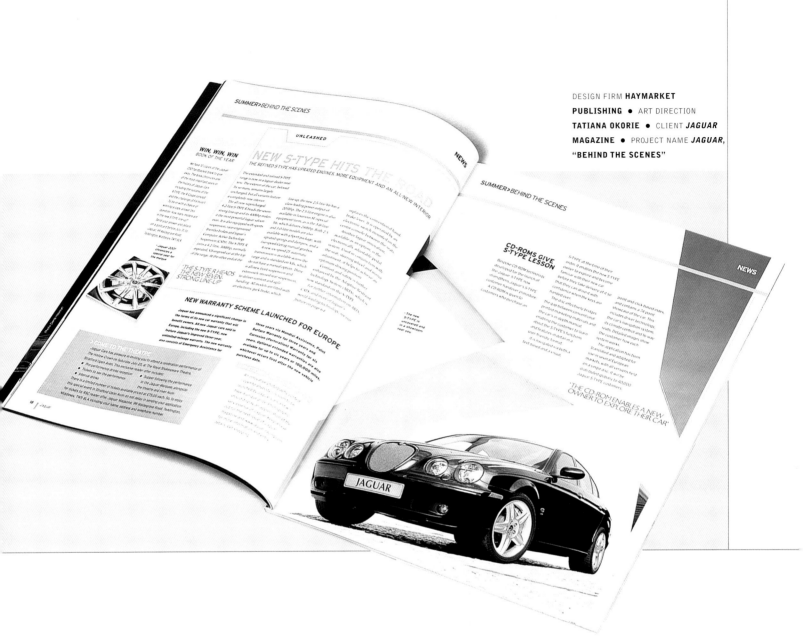

DESIGN FIRM **HAYMARKET
PUBLISHING** ● ART DIRECTION
TATIANA OKORIE ● CLIENT *JAGUAR*
MAGAZINE ● PROJECT NAME *JAGUAR,*
"BEHIND THE SCENES"

One of the most challenging aspects of magazine design has to be the demands of handling sections containing a medley of small articles within a limited space. Each minifeature must have its own space and, to a certain degree, its own identity, while still firmly belonging to the whole of the section. Within "Behind the Scenes," Tatiana Okorie has successfully filled the available space with a fusion of varied textures and tones. Each individual article is presented in a different manner, shifting color and typographic priorities, while maintaining a sense of compatibility with the complete page.

DESIGN FIRM **STUDIO VERTEX** ●
DESIGN **KAREN CHENG, MICHAEL**
LINDSAY ● CLIENT **SIMPSON CENTER**
● PROJECT *SIMPSON NEWSLETTER*

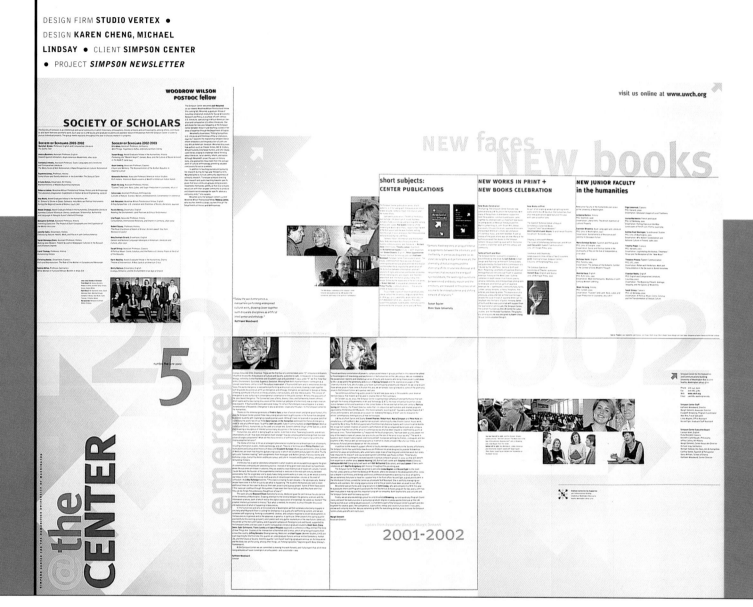

Working on the newsletter for Simpson Center, part of the University of Washington in Seattle, involves dealing with a huge amount of copy. "LAST MINUTE TEXT ADDITIONS REQUIRED THE ELIMINATION OF ANY LARGE-SCALE IMAGERY," says Michael Lindsey of Studio Vertex, "SO WE GENERATED A MORE TYPOGRAPHIC POSTER, USING DESCRIPTIONS AND HEADINGS TO CREATE VISUAL INTEREST." A strong grid structure provides cohesion, while changes of typographic line spacing, column widths, and point sizes create textural and tonal diversity. Tight arrangements of subject-specific information allow for comfortable areas of space that make reading easier and more enticing, and the clever use of two-color overprinting in different ways gives the illusion of a less budget-conscious job.

DESIGN FIRM **JOHN BROWN CITRUS
PUBLISHING** ● ART DIRECTION
JEREMY LESLIE ● CLIENT *M-REAL*
MAGAZINE ● PROJECT NAME *M-REAL*

Words. The third in a series of magazines that challenge our perceptions. Featuring Ed Fella, Torin Douglas, Jonathan Fenby, Jen Dugan, Lewis Blackwell, Gary Cook, and David Eldridge. It is a magazine like no other. It is nameless and indefinable – what you see is what you get.

Euro 3.70
GBE 3.50
US$ 5.50
Issue 3

As with other issues of this exciting magazine, issue 3 is contained within a "belly band" and is entirely devoted to one topic, in this case, words. It is interesting to note that both the restraining strip and cover totally embrace the principle of "considerable information within limited space."

The magenta band contains six lines of lightweight copy in white, cyan, and yellow. This sans serif type has a large X-height and is closely leaded, filling the space totally. On the cover below, we are treated to a totally different scale of text, and with the aid of a magnifying glass, the viewer is able to read the copy that is to be found contained within the magazine. Again, using just cyan, magenta, and yellow we see sans serif type that totally fills the space, but however, this time, overlaid and at an extremely reduced size.

143

DESIGN FIRM **JOHN BROWN CITRUS**
PUBLISHING ● ART DIRECTION
JEREMY LESLIE ● CLIENT **IKEA**
● PROJECT NAME **ROOM**

ISSUE 19 CONTAINS...

Striking use of color and pattern epitomizes the contents sections for this issue of *Room*. The grid is accentuated by the use of colored blocks, which divide the pages and flow behind text. San serif typography produces an interesting textural mix of scale and hue that fills space with little room to spare.

Annual Review 2000

The unusual format of this annual review is surprisingly revealed upon opening the cover, when fourteen accordion-fold pages filled with information spill out. All pages utilize a four-column grid that simply and effectively caters to this mass of text. In order to lessen the impact of the columns, Furnell and Felton printed most copy using a light gray ink, highlighting certain areas with a vivid red. Combining this typographic approach with cut-out imagery has the effect of increasing the readers' awareness of space, while in many ways hiding the fact that this report has a lot to say.

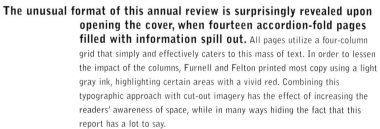

DESIGN FIRM **FELTON COMMUNICATIONS** ● ART DIRECTION **ROGER FELTON** ● DESIGN **BRION FURNELL** ● COPY **RICHARD SCHOLEY** ● CLIENT **PRESS COMPLAINTS COMMISSION** ● PROJECT NAME *PRESS COMPLAINTS COMMISSION ANNUAL REVIEW*

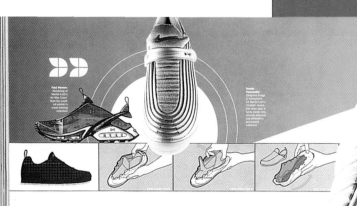

"What if your
shoes could
be planted—
the seeds of
your next pair?
I have three
kids, I'd like
to leave them
something that's
important to me.
Plantable shoes."

"innovation requires a dedication beyond reason...

...It's a religion."

because they are no longer relevant to consumers. If you're trained to be an architect or industrial designer or graphic designer, the same creative philosophy and principles that you apply to your home discipline are absolutely appropriate to everything else. You can see that within the last decade. Products remind me of miniature buildings. Buildings remind me of clothing. Clothing reminds me of a car and vice versa. So there's a lot of excitement there because the traditional boundaries have been blurred and hopefully will eventually erase. **If you put an architect, fashion designer and product designer to work on a car, you will come up with very different solutions. New products, hybrid products. A huge potential to collaborate.** Before I came to Nike I worked for an architect named Michael Graves for about four years. I showed up to Michael Graves' doorstep, basically penniless with a huge ability to work. And it blew me away that an architect was working on a small scale—tea kettles and things. It was an epiphany: "Oh, yeah, you can apply your design ethos to anything." Michael Graves cleared the path for me. He was a painter. He did theatrical shows, apparel, products. He did houses, buildings, did it all. **I think that's how all designers should work. The shoe I just designed was inspired by the Guggenheim Bilbao.** That building looks like a spacecraft landed in Bilbao, in this old city, and I really wanted to do this same thing with the shoe—make a spaceship that landed in the footwear stores. That's one of the beautiful things about being a designer. You take in a bunch of information and then make these odd connections. And oftentimes those connections create hybrid concepts. **Architecture, fashion and industrial design are intertwined. But so often they're created as separate units. We experience it as a system; let's design them together as a system. It makes logical sense that those disciplines come closer and inspire each other to do**

better things. When Frank Lloyd Wright designed one property, he designed the plates on the table, and the kitchen, and the suit and the dress that the [homeowners] wore when they first walked in. He said this is the way life should always be, this connection between the plate and the dress and the house. The integration is going to help all the disciplines, and help us become a much richer creative society. **It's like making a puzzle piece. We haven't really brought them together to create the entire picture. Of course, for me, the human body is always the point where everything starts. We try to mimic what the foot is doing and learn from that and apply it specifically.** The notion of 'biomimicry' makes a lot of sense. Human beings have their feet, eyesight, sweat glands... If we're not innovating in ways that help amplify the positive aspects, we're not doing much. Mother nature is the best designer out there. She's had like 6 billion years to go back and redesign. We talk about modern design—simplicity and streamlining. Apply those principles to a butterfly wing. There's a ton that can be learned there. The cross between a modern aesthetic and nature... Ergonomics is a way to help inform that design decision. A lot of designers 'say less is more.' I think to a certain degree with Nike that's true, because we are

trying to refine the products we sell, boil it down to what's absolutely necessary, and craft in a way that's not just functional but beautiful. Knowing what to exclude is a really big part of design. **That's really how I approach every design. I say, 'What's the icon of the shoe?' You need to have one focal point. In the past, we have done so many shoes with so much stuff on it, just not really organized, no hierarchy. You should have a hierarchy, a focal point, a key component.** If I had all the time in the world and was asked to redesign something that just sucks, it would be a coach class airline seat. I think they are an abomination. Everything you just talked about, it just follows the direct opposite discourse. So I would design a seat that is based on the human form and figure. And make the entire experience of sitting on an airplane a lot more human. **There are definitely lots of problems to solve.** Do you think we should eventually stop designing? Is there a time when you can no longer reinvent the wheel? **Not as long as you see design as problem solving. I don't think you will ever get to the point where you have no more problems to solve.** For me, stopping designing would be like turning off your imagination. It's just an inherent part of our species that we desire to create, to change the future. Stopping would basically be the death of our society, the death of our species. But does an object ever reach a pinnacle? I think it's a totally differ-

ent question, because I also believe that there are some incredible examples of design that are just a perfect balance of all you need and all you don't. Certain pieces just stand the test of time. **And still look good.** That damn pencil sharpener from Raymond Loewy. Or Charles Eames' chair, the pinnacle expression of the chair. Doing that in a different color, why? Doing that in a different material? Why would you do that? It's done, it's baked. Let it alone. **What does the nike swoosh represent to you?** I believe the swoosh is an important signal that represents people innovating for other people. It stands for innovation, confidence and ultimately human potential. As a graphic symbol, it communicates a position globally without the boundaries of language.

How will the branding and symbols become more subtle or more subliminal? I think oftentimes we've saturated the messaging of the symbol, by having it appear too pronounced or too many times. I believe in a much more subtle, refined approach to branding. The swoosh is the punctuation of the vision of the company.

I do think that branding will continue to be somewhat paradoxical in the next couple of decades: Symbols serve a function of individual expression. You buy a product that you believe in, and at the same time you want to be by yourself, to be viewed as who you are, not just what you're wearing. >

143

DESIGN FIRM **EXQUISITE
CORPORATION** ● DESIGN **RILEY
JOHN-DONNELL** ● COPY **JEREMY LIN**
● CLIENT *SURFACE* MAGAZINE
● PROJECT NAME *SURFACE*

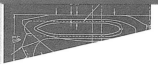

Sound Track:
Nike's cross
training top
with built-in
mp3 player

"The consumers' appetite for what's next is Nike's fuel."

Feats of Glory:
John Hoke's
Niketown London
features the 'Joy of
Play' chandelier &
photos of young
local athletes;
Hoke's Nike Park
boasts the 'Retail
Cone,' displaying
400 soccer boots,
World Cup trophy &
interactive displays

Visual signals link consumers to a point of view. Brands definitely connect a philosophy to a product. I think that's very important. But as the culture seeks out opportunities to gain further individual expression, brand symbols sometimes represent uniformity and commercialization. This battle for acceptance and independence will continue. **For me, the swoosh represents innovation, inspiration, exploring new territories—as well as authenticity. And yet it's unpredictable: You never know what Nike will come up with next. It exemplifies 'just do it.' It can vary from very minimal to in-your-face. Currently I'm definitely into the subtle approach.** What distinguishes an innovation from a gimmick? **That's actually a fairly simple one. An innovative product addresses a specific need. If it solves a problem, it will enhance the performance of athletes. If you solve a problem, you will not end up with a gimmick.** Innovation requires a commitment to three things: Research, failure and more research. Innovation requires a dedication beyond reason. Innovation is a religion; I guess the belief is in yourself— trusting in your intuition and your instinct. I also believe innovation is about making history and inspiring people. Innovation is using your imagination. Innovation is about the future. A gimmick is about selling, lying and transacting. A gimmick is shit. **If a company stands for innovation, it's hard to stand still. Nike reinvents itself every four months with each launch of a new collection. I think that's a real challenge and a fantastic opportunity for designers.** I've always believed that Nike is synonymous with change. We can't rely on the successes of our

"Architecture, fashion & industrial design are intertwined... But they're created as separate units. We experience it as a system— let's design as a system. The disciplines should come together & inspire each other to do better things."

past. Innovating as a rule destroys comfort and stability. Innovation is often about pure chaos. From chaos great ideas are born. Comfort and consistency breed complacency and boredom, which equals the death of new ideas, which equals you're fucked, you're dead. If it's about evolution versus revolution, Nike is about revolution. **We are all part of this revolution. Finding the next big thing is the true challenge.** The thing I love about revolution is that the king doesn't start it, all the people below the king do. The patriots start revolution. So we're kind of the patriots of design. **Nike is embroiled in controversies over its production methods. Can the designs of a shoe inform more**

eco-friendly, people-friendly means of manufacture? This is a very timely issue and something the company takes very seriously. I think in many ways the design staff is becoming more interested, and responsible, to make a product that is environmentally friendly. And a product that is easy to build. The creative staff will be forced to consider all the implications of the design, and that's new. We need to know that the products we create have implications on the manufacturing floor, on the environment, on shipping, packaging. All those constraints and concerns. I'd love to see our designers create history by solving all these issues. If the design staff can start tackling the way products are assembled, or the way materials can be reused, rethought or reinterpreted... It means designing cradle to grave, all the way to the ground. **It's really looking at the entire life of a product, from the first time you put pen to paper. It's the responsibility of the designer to think that way, and I don't think in the past we have addressed that, period.**

I would love to see products that actually have a life span... That could be disposed of in the ground, buried, and be completely biodegradable. I'd like to think of our products' end as an opportunity to transform into something new. I was just thinking it would be cool if you could actually plant your shoes, actually take it out into the garden and plant it into the ground. A couple seasons later, an ear of corn comes up. What if you could create shoes that became the seeds of the next shoe? It reminded me of when Native Americans would bury fish with the corn seed. The fish was like a fertilizer, and they used to throw the corn in the river to catch the fish—a cycle. I thought it would be cool if there was a place where Nike took it all back, huge fields in Oregon. 'There's a basketball shoe growing some hemp. There's the running shoe, growing some tofu.' I think that would be really fantastic. Since I have three kids, I'd like to leave them something that's important to me. Plantable shoes. **Imagine if your apparel went from a passive object to become active, so it would give you feedback. I think Nike is in the position to pull it off.** Is it frustrating that consumers are always looking for the next big thing? **No, no, no! It's really the best thing that could happen. It pushes us. It's a designer's dream to work in an industry that serves a market that demands new technology** (Continued on page 188)

When complex page layouts containing lots of text and imagery come together really well, it is impossible to describe in a few succinct words precisely how and why this is! So many design decisions are responsible for providing visual cohesion and content coherence without being static or predictable. In these pages, changes of scale, mixes of photography and illustration, and squared-up imagery overlapped by cutouts all create visible attractions for the viewer, while consistency of colors, shapes, typefaces, alignments, and angles ensures a kind of comforting familiarity.

▣ DREAM DEBUT

3.45PM, MARCH 3, 2002. THE TEAM GOES
WILD AS MIKA SALO CROSSES THE LINE,
SCORING TOYOTA'S VERY FIRST WORLD
CHAMPIONSHIP POINT ON ITS FORMULA 1
DEBUT IN MELBOURNE, AUSTRALIA...

WORDS: OLIVER PEAGAM • PHOTOGRAPHY: KARL GRANT

DESIGN FIRM **HAYMARKET
PUBLISHING** • ART DIRECTION **BEN
MARTIN** • COPY **OLIVER PEAGAM** •
PHOTOGRAPHY **CARL GRANT** • CLIENT
TOYOTA • PROJECT NAME ***ONE AIM,***
"DREAM DEBUT"

We debated long and hard as to where would be the most appropriate location to show "Dream Debut," and have settled upon this section for a number of reasons. "Dream Debut" is fundamentally a diary, recording in tremendous detail Formula One's newest team at their debut in Australia. This is by no means a traditional format for a diary. Minimal text describes the many behind-the-scenes action shots, while tremendously detailed photography captures and explains the minutia of daily events. Within this article, comprehensive photography covers every millimeter of the spread. Ultimately, the amount of verbal but mainly visual language in "Dream Debut," firmly ensures its position within the second section of this book.

"Ask a hundred music devotees what their favorite late-night LP is, and chances are you'll get a hundred different answers," begins the copy on this spread, and that is exactly what has been listed across both pages. Far from being tedious and visually unexciting however, the layout celebrates a distinct contrast from all other pages in the publication with an allover bleed black background and strong electric blue blocks of text reversed through. There is virtually no space available for any form of embellishment, leaving the type itself as image in a very arresting fabriclike pattern. Two white boxes contain the editorial text, and although it is probably unlikely that many, if any, will read the hundred favorite LPs, the effect gives a visual enjoyment that makes an excellent substitute.

DESIGN FIRM **JOHN BROWN CITRUS PUBLISHING** ● ART DIRECTION **WARREN JACKSON** ● DESIGN **JEREMY LESLIE, RICHARD SPELLMAN** ● CLIENT **VIRGIN ATLANTIC** ● PROJECT NAME *HOT AIR*, **"LATE JUNCTION"**

DESIGN FIRM **Z3** ● DESIGN
SCOTT RAYBOULD ● COPY **WEST
MIDLANDS LIFE** ● CLIENT
WEST MIDLANDS LIFE ● PROJECT
NAME **CULTURAL IDEAS GUIDE**

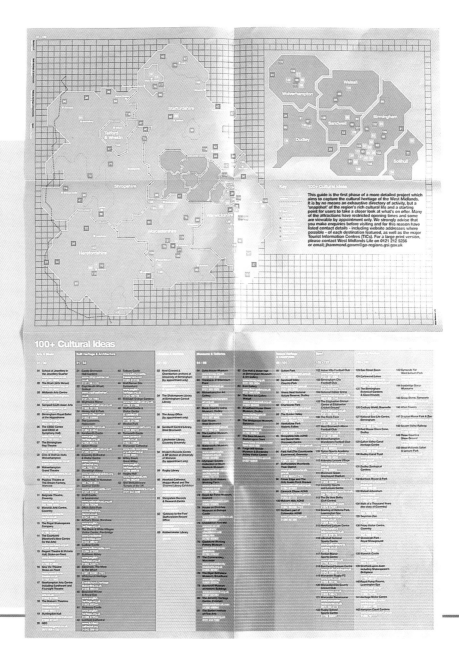

"A hundred and one plus" cultural ideas from the West Midlands of the U.K. are included on this 23.5" × 15.5" (59.4 cm × 42 cm) broadsheet, with photographs, descriptions, locations, and contacts presented in an interesting and accessible manner. On one side, narrow strips of varying-scale photography introduce visual vitality, with a ten-column grid aiding organization and clarity. On the reverse, exciting color relationships code the cultural categories, providing listings and locations in a layout that captures contemporary style and yet is suitable for all ages. Most distinctively, a fifth color, silver, is used throughout as a bleed background, giving the impression that the piece is printed on double-sided silver stock.

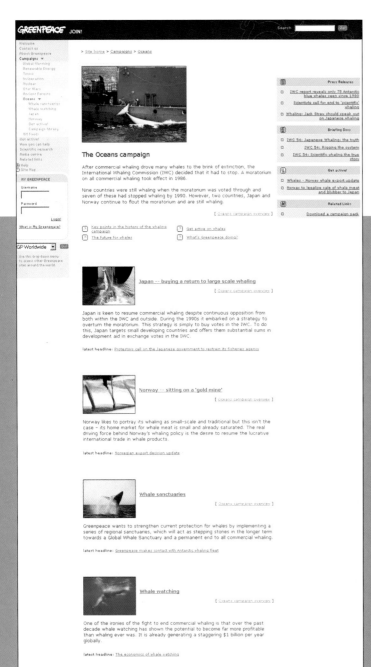

DESIGN FIRM **RECHORD** ● ART DIRECTION **STEFAN CARTWRIGHT RACHEL COLLINSON** ● DESIGN **LOUISE CARRIER** ● CLIENT **GREENPEACE U.K.** ● PROJECT NAME **GREENPEACE UK WEB SITE, WWW.GREENPEACE.ORG.UK**

"THIS BRIEF WAS ENTIRELY DAUNTING," explains Rachel Collinson of Rechord. "WE WERE ASKED TO REDESIGN THE SITE, MAKE IT USABLE WITHOUT ALIENATING ANY SUPPORTERS WHO MIGHT BE USING OLDER TECHNOLOGY FOR ENVIRONMENTAL REASONS, AND GIVE A SENSE OF ORDER TO THE CONSIDERABLE 'SOUP' OF DOCUMENTS THAT HAVE OUTGROWN THE INTERFACE!"

Without making the site confusing by giving the viewer too much to look at all at once, Rechord's solution presents the audience with a choice of navigation options, breaking the available information down into manageable chunks. The layout automatically fills the viewer's monitor and includes design devices known as "context relevant modules," which link through discreet icons to documents that are pertinent to the subject matter of the page.

DESIGN FIRM **WAGNER DESIGN** ●
ART DIRECTION **JILL WAGNER** ●
PRODUCTION **AMY ZAPAWA** ● COPY
LINDA FITZGERALD ● CLIENT
**MICHIGAN DEPARTMENT OF
EDUCATION** ● PROJECT NAME **30
IDEAS IN 30 DAYS BROCHURE**

For the newly appointed superintendent of public education in Michigan, Wagner Design has put together this fourteen-page accordion-fold leaflet that sets out thirty ideas for improving the public education system. "THE CONCEPT PLAYS ON THE IDEA THAT THERE IS MUCH TO DO IN EDUCATION, AND VERY LITTLE TIME OR RESOURCES TO ACCOMPLISH IT," says Jill Wagner. Each idea is separately grouped and headed by dramatic numbering; all the available space is used to the fullest extent, and pages are packed with information, including quotes, a diversity of imagery, and bright colors.

WORDS IN SPACE

Neal Kane | President | Libretto

For the designer, text can represent an opportunity or an intrusion. Graphic spaces, both print and online, are often made or broken by the words they display. Having collaborated with designers for more than 15 years, I thought it would be helpful to share a few of the techniques my company uses to help enhance collaboration among designers, writers, and clients.

BREATHING ROOM

One of the most important considerations in determining how words exist within the graphic space is page count. This is particularly true with print, where projects must grow (or contract) in cumbersome, four-page increments. When bidding a project with a designer, we often hear, "The client wants to limit the capabilities brochure to six pages, since they don't want it to be too long."

While the desire for brevity is understandable, especially in these days of often-threadbare budgets, "lowballing" page count can seriously compromise a project, or ruin it altogether. While it's tempting to envision the finished piece as a physical object, it makes better sense to first gain a sense of what the client is trying to accomplish, and then structure format accordingly. The ultimate goal is a collaborative process in which the client, designer, and writer jointly determine how much story there is to tell, and how much space is required to make the resulting piece both readable and affordable.

Take the example of the six-page capabilities brochure. The same piece can easily be reconfigured into an undersized eight-page, saddle-stitched piece that offers the "thud factor" of a booklet, and enables the writer/designer team to construct a complete story — all while consuming less paper.

If the client needs an entire collateral program, a logical page count also creates a sense of hierarchy between pieces: eight to twelve pages for a capabilities piece, four to six pages for product literature, two pages for case studies, etc. Again, the goal is to "right-size" each piece in terms of the story it has to convey and its place among other elements within the program.

KILLER HEADLINES

One of the most effective visual presentation techniques a designer can use is actually verbal: incorporating "real" headlines into sample covers and spreads. For clients trying to evaluate one direction against another, a lucid headline can do an enormous amount to bridge the gap between the presentation board and the finished piece. Well-articulated headlines also demonstrate that the creative team understands the client's top-level "talking points."

Several years ago, we were collaborating with Raincastle Communications on the first annual report for an IT consulting firm. One of the ideas the creative team brainstormed centered on the theme "Looking Back, Facing Front." In the client presentation, FPO photographs were included showing the front and back of human figures, along with headlines that used the words "front" and "back" to illustrate the company's core capabilities and values:

The companies that will emerge at the front of the electronic business market are those that best leverage their back-end systems.

The team-building activities that we conduct at the front end of engagements provide a strategic advantage that delivers back-end results.

During the presentation, there was a sense of palpable relief among members of the client team, who saw that much of their complex service offering could be summed up in several sentences using a simple verbal device. A number of those "front" and "back" headlines made their way into the finished, award-winning piece.

WORDS IN VIRTUAL SPACE

When it comes to working with text for online applications, some rules carry over from the print world – and many don't. Because people tend to "scan" Web pages instead of reading in depth, the writer should play an active role in minimizing online word count where possible. Designers bidding these projects should consider enlisting the services of a writing resource to address the factors that arise in creating or adapting Web content, in areas that include:

- Refining site architecture to determine which pages will require a greater or lesser amount of text
- Crafting compelling copy for Flash introductions, home pages and rollovers
- Repurposing print materials for the online medium to reflect a balance between the client's online and offline marketing needs, and to improve online readability
- Creating or reviewing button names

FLOURISHES AND FINE-TUNING

Over the course of a project, there are many areas where collaboration between the writer and designer can add value and elegance to the finished piece. When estimating the hours for a project, leave yourself time to address factors with the writer that streamline workflow and improve quality:

- Establishing a rough word count as early as possible to facilitate layout design
- Working with the writer to determine how his or her understanding of the client's business can enhance your choice of themes and images
- Collaborating with the writer to enhance the piece through sidebars, callouts, captions, subheads, and other techniques
- Obtain an early draft of the copy for any longer piece, such as a brochure, read it in its entirety, and share your feedback with the writer with regard to its "designability"

We often say that a successful project requires three elements: a great designer, a great writer, and a great client. Employing these techniques can help you and your firm play an active role in leveraging the power of words to create extraordinary work.

Neal Kane is the president of Libretto, a Boston-based provider of strategic writing services that include naming and branding, annual reports, websites, and print and multimedia communications. He is a former AIGA/Boston board member and currently serves on the chapter's Advisory Board.

05/10

James Billiter
Freelance Designer
Cincinatti, OH

SPATIAL USAGE FROM URBAN TO RURAL

One day at lunch I went up to the Observation Deck of the Carew Tower, Cincinnati's largest skyscraper. I noticed that there were several stages from urban to rural. I created a series of photos comparing and contrasting spatial usage in the different stages of urban, suburban, and rural. Using a family of graphic symbols I attempted to mirror the selected environment. The designs were printed on acetate and placed in front of the scene when photographed.

The first photo uses the graphic elements to capitalize on the visual flatness of the rural landscape. The second photo illustrates the seemingly never-ending repetitive nature of the suburbs. The graphic elements become more dense. The third photo shows a small urban city center, where intersections become more intense and there is more congestion. The fourth photo illustrates the extreme perspective that one feels when two street corners intersect.

space (sp[=a]s), n.
a quantity or portion of distance from one thing to another, interval between two or more objects.

"Space" is the theme of this premier issue of the American Institute of Graphic Arts journal, and it is explored from as many angles as possible. The pages are a sophisticated integration of conventional design systems with a considerably more unusual and personalized usage of tints, shaped picture boxes, and graphic rules. "I USED TOOLS SUCH AS BARS OF COLOR TO EMPHASIZE CALL-OUTS WHEN ROOM DIDN'T ALLOW FOR THAT MUCH WHITE SPACE OR A DIFFERENCE IN FONT SIZE," says Kjerstin Westgaard, "AND I WORKED STRICTLY WITH THE GRID TO MAKE SURE ITEMS REMAINED ORGANIZED DESPITE THE LARGE AMOUNT OF INFORMATION." These practical concerns are then skillfully complemented by more playful and experimental angles and shapes that frame or present images and text to create powerful and enticing layouts.

DESIGN FIRM **AIGA BOSTON CHAPTER** ● DESIGN **KJERSTIN WESTGAARD** ● COPY **ALISON NOBLE** ● ILLUSTRATION **KJERSTIN WESTGAARD** ● CLIENT **AIGA BOSTON CHAPTER** ● PROJECT NAME ***JOURNAL OF AIGA BOSTON***

ROOM SERVICE

Students from Gerhard Schønning High School in Trondheim, Norway were the artists behind this installation project. Their task was to plan an installation using only the materials provided. An empty classroom and meeting room were provided for the project. Working in groups of four the students were given keywords such as: open/closed, vertical/horizontal, light/dark, inside/outside, high/low, hiding place/labyrinth, material/contrast/proportion, and space/experience to base their design on. Each installation had to be self-supporting, without the use of glue, tape or other adhesive. The students worked together to construct the two models that were chosen from the class (only one is featured on the left).

Kenn Boostrom | Visual Executive Office | Hotwire Design

Kenn Boostrom owns Hotwire Design in Providence, RI, a firm specializing in planning, identity and product launch services. He has been duly noted in Print Magazine, Graphis and Mead Top 60.

THE SCIENTIFIC DEATH OF WHITE SPACE

Designers have traditionally used white space to help guide a reader's eyes, onto and through print ads. Recent scientific research into how the human eye moves and views a page, however, seems to suggest that image trumps space.

The Verify Corporation in the Netherlands is using new laser technology, to track eye movement and the amount of time an eye spends following a composition. Using more than 100 points per second (signified by red dots), Verify tracks and plots, the navigation of the eye. The technology checks the composition of an advertisement, and shows, if an eye passes over the brand name or logo.

In spread after spread, myself and a dozen other designers, were privileged to see the visual charting of eye movements. Spreads and single-page ads were consistently riddled with red dots, starting at the target element in the spread. The red dots swept in from top to bottom, and left or right depending upon the composition, but eye move-ment always originated at the top of the page. Creating a virtual map, the dots spread apart and clustered in and around the image area of original focus. Then, moving on, the dots follow a path to the next area of interest.

In all laser tracking tests, men and women were tested with the same viewing material. Men and women followed the composition in the same pattern. Anytime that human skin appeared in the ad, all eyes looked with extreme accuracy at the same areas. Obviously, this was not the focus of the test but a very interesting result nonetheless. The test results demonstrate that human interest, eyes, and whether or not they scan the brand name or logo. White space was never an issue on laser tracking - the eye always originates at the top and zeroes in on the target element.

The scientific evidence points to a new understanding of ways to improve print design and communication. With this new technology, companies can better test their print ads prior to publication. The layout, and ads tested were compositionally very diverse. In every case, both men's and women's eyes travelled quickly over white, black and red space and focused on photography and typography. Eyes, it seems, travel without prejudice. In the end, eyes were focused on image rather than white space (and a little skin often provided the focal point).

Reference:
Mr Geert Framsen,
Managing Director
Verify Corporation Nederland.

06/10

William Peebles
Product Designer
Columbus, OH

SUBURBAN SPRAWL

Many areas around here don't have any developments and when I see a new one I am drawn to it. Not because it is beautiful but because it doesn't belong. The deer tracks on top of the bulldozer tracks are a reminder of whose space this really is. I enjoy my modern conveniences, but do we really need another Wal mart? Especially when there is one less than a mile away. Convenience and expansion have become top priority, and things that really matter take a back seat. It is painful to witness in eight months the fall of farm land that could feed thousands and the rise of ultra suburban homes built by mega builders eventually taking its place. Most of which remain empty. Dead space.

338

BLACKLICK SQUARE
Chinese Restaurant
Beer Wine Drive-Thru
Dick Pick

LEGIBILITY

SEEING WORDS

The miracle of being able to read and write, usually taken for granted, is something most people rarely re-examine in adult life.

Type can take a back seat so that the reader hardly registers it, or it can shout loud and demand to be noticed. Whichever view you take, legibility is key, says Graham Vickers

PAGE TWENTY-FOUR

Few of us can remember exactly how we learned to read, and the quantum leap from communication by sounds to communication through graphic symbols is, in general, a happily accepted but largely unconsidered fact of life. Most people only begin to think about the subject when they suddenly encounter a context where the presentation of those graphic symbols poses problems of perception – when text becomes illegible, unreadable or impossible to navigate. We may consider legibility to be a failure of the eye-brain to decode a given word or symbol; readability, on the other hand, is more to do with the formatting and organisation of words to create accessible text.

Why do such problems of perception still arise? After all, given the long history of type, would it not be reasonable to suppose that most of the fundamental difficulties of typographic communication would have long since been ironed out? There are two basic reasons why difficulties seem to be endemic in the graphic representation of words. One has to do with the nature of the typographer's role – a role defined by both the individual personalities involved and, historically speaking, by the permanently inflexible job descriptions and relationships between typographer, printer and print designer or on-screen designer. The other is that, despite the unchanging physical capacity of the human eye and brain, the way in which we process visual information changes all the time, and never

faster or more radically than during the past 20 years. Prevailing technology and the visual manners of any age mean that we are constantly relearning how to interpret visual information of every kind, and that includes the written word.

To ask the question "What is the typographer's role in all this?" is to open a very large can of worms. Stating the case for transparency, British-based American typographer Beatrice Warde (1900-1969) declared that classical typography had demonstrated itself to be an ideal "clearly polished window" through which ideas could be communicated. She believed that type **should be invisible and that the designer/typographer existed not for the purpose of expressing personal design preferences, but to provide an** unobtrusive link between author and reader. At the other end of the scale, there is the quite reasonable argument that type can and does also convey something variously referred to as "atmosphere", "feel" or "impress", something that establishes a sense of anticipation regarding the contents or purpose of the page. This option may be used responsibly or otherwise. It

may be deployed subtly to underpin the desired mood, or it may be taken as licence to play avant-garde tricks that treat blocks of type as little more than pictorial elements on the page, with scant regard for legibility – ideas seen "through a glass, darkly" as opposed to "through a clearly polished window".

How, then, are they to be identified, these basic criteria that let us distinguish and follow words on the page or screen?

Richard Hollis, noted typographer and author of Graphic Design: A Concise History (Thames & Hudson, 1994), maintains that at one point legibility became a particularly vexing issue for a particular age-group of typographers.

"Because my generation was brought up with fixed type in the 1960s, we began to feel that

Looking at the text

Each of your eyes contains 130 million light receptors. Each of these can take in at least five photons per second.

Images are decoded in the retinal neurones, sent along the optic nerve and transmitted to the occipital lobe at the back of the head. The brain directs your eyes to follow the pattern of words on the page. When reading, the two cannot follow a smooth line on the page; instead it jumps along the text line, stopping ...

The speed of reading

... of each letter, are easier to read from paper than sans serif faces, which do not have serifs. This is because it is believed that serifs help distinguish each individual letter. Others, tyI4().

Much of the published research on optimization of reading has been done with paper media. Research on reading from paper media has yielded the following results (Frenckin, K. 1991, Legibility of continuous text on computer screens – a guide to the ...

---

but we survive. And still people keep on inventing new typefaces."

Hollis concludes that, in spite of passing fashion, certain designs recommend themselves simply because they are so easy to read. "Despite all the innovation, people continue to use the same fundamental typefaces as they did in the 18th century. You had a standardised object that nobody has changed basically, and, with some slight variation, it still works. In the same way, newspaper faces today are all more or less the same. But there is always the will to do **new: novelty for novelty's sake. I wonder what the interest is for people to develop new typefaces, particularly now that it's so difficult to control copyright, but it's always there... a kind of mania.** Perhaps the acid test for typographic legibility and readability is the design of telephone directories and dictionaries. Here, no one is interested in modish typographic adventures, but simply in conveying large amounts of information accessibly and in the smallest practical space. This is where legibility is tested by the empirical method: if people cannot easily find telephone numbers or locate the lexicographical information they

need, an expensive product has failed badly. When, in the 1960s, the British designer Colin Banks reworked the American Bell directory system for the UK telephone books, part of his client's motivation was a saving of literally millions of pounds in production costs. Banks increased the x-height and produced a four-column page and removed nonverbal surnames (instead of 200 repetitions of the surname "Smith", the name now appeared just once with all the relative forenames and initials listed below). In conjunction with tweaking the letter forms for the purpose of reproduction, these simple (by making smaller missions into spaces that were inclined to fill up during firing), Banks succeeded in simultaneously addressing several key aspects of legibility: exploiting the most beneficial x-height; shortening the horizontal distance the eye has to travel before **returning to the beginning of the next line** (a process known as doubling); and testing traditional assumptions about organising information.

Professor Paul Luna of Reading University is engaged in research into dictionary design, where entities must not only be easy to find, but quite elaborate hierarchies of lexicographical information also need to be present.

"Certainly, dense amounts of text have to be navigated," he says, "but also the nature of this particular sort of text is telegraphic in that practically every word in a string may need some differentiation – a part of speech indicator, a variant form or whatever."

Ironically, these issues were once tackled in a very effective way rarely available to the contemporary print dictionary

typefaces like Verdana, but if you're doing a bold or italic, you've always got the pixel structure to cope with." Luna says. "Anti-aliasing technology has improved things to some extent, but pixel structure is still a constraint on the degree to which you can embolden or italicise. You're talking about relatively crude increments of angle and curve compared to what you can achieve on paper."

Anti-aliasing, with its now familiar device of introducing intermediate grey pixels to trick the eye into seeing a curve or oblique stroke that otherwise looks too jagged, has **recently been improved upon, at least for a particular** context. If certain characters are ugly to read on a regular Cathode Ray Tube (CRT) screen, the challenge of the full-screen laptop or hand-held device is even greater. In an effort to stimulate the practice of reading e-books on such portable devices, Microsoft developed ClearType™, a process that uses sub-pixel anti-aliasing. Put simply, this improves the usual method of on-screen font rendering (which assumes that each tiny black square pixel is either "on" or "off", so giving rise to jagged letters), modifying the area beyond the traditional pixel boundary by

triggering just one of the three available beam lines.

Malcolm Garrett of London-based interactive communications agency AMX has long experience of working with type in a changing visual culture. He is wary of treating the phenomenon of text on screen too radically.

"Just because we have new media for looking at words, it doesn't mean we have to develop a new 'paradigm' or a 'new language'," he says. "In terms of the Web, I'm quite critical of sites that describe themselves as intuitive – when what they actually mean is unintelligible."

Garrett identifies what he sees as an inappropriate

... factors to consider when printing text

• Small serif light faces, particularly serif fonts in colours that mix more than one or two process colours, are difficult to reproduce. The same applies to small-sized reverse text on a coloured background.

• Cannot printing differs from offset, as black text also consists of halftone cells. The screen's look slightly ragged, whereas in offset printing all areas are black. Halftones also make greyish printing more sensitive to delicate fonts when only black (or other single-process colour) is used.

• Light fonts in small sizes require a good-quality paper to reproduce correctly. Coated papers produce better than uncoated. Special grades with a rough or textured surface are not compatible with fine detail. But when a more standard overprint-grade overperforms computer screens in its ability to reproduce small text ...

MEDIUM, NOT FOR HIS OR HER OWN IDEAL MEDIUM, AND THAT PROBLEM OF SCREEN RESOLUTION IS EXACERBATED AT THE INTERACTIVE TV STAGE WITH ITS CRUDER RESOLUTION. AGAIN IT DEMANDS APPROPRIATE SOLUTIONS.

INSTEAD OF FRETTING TOO MUCH ABOUT ISSUES OF RESOLUTION, GARRATT WOULD RATHER EXPLORE THE POSSIBILITIES OF THE ONE GENUINELY SIGNIFICANT DIMENSION THAT THE NEW MEDIA

bring to the display of words: time.

"Because the major difference is time itself, legibility can be controlled or aided by the pace at which things reveal themselves to the screen," he says. "The order in which information comes up, plus the speed and the logic applied to delivering that information, can be extremely helpful in terms of legibility."

He quotes one of the Web's most famous sites as a negative example. "You go to a site like Amazon or one of those being album-in-commerce sites, and the screen is just full of information. You kind of suspect that everything you need is there, but there's no real help to find your way around the screen, no hierarchical presentation of information."

He concludes: "Now, conventional print designers have been pretty good at organising information page by page. If they could extend that skill and bring to it some of the skill a broadcaster has in using time to reveal information in a particular order, you might at last have something that is genuinely intuitive and at the same time quite useful, informative and legible." ∎

With the advantages of on-screen readability come potential disadvantages of aesthetics and legibility, not least in the limited options available to render bold and italic variants.

You can use very legible on-screen

Graham Vickers is a London-based freelance writer specialising in digital media and design

---

DESIGN FIRM **JOHN BROWN CITRUS PUBLISHING** ● ART DIRECTION **JEREMY LESLIE** ● COPY **GRAHAM VICKERS** ● CLIENT **M-REAL MAGAZINE** ● PROJECT NAME **M-REAL**

Exploring the miracle of reading and writing, this issue on the theme of "legibility" crams many of its pages with a variety of type. Copy is divided into same-size sections and interpreted in a multitude of ways, with a patchwork effect throughout. Changes from one texture to another occur midsentence, perpetuating the pattern qualities of the layout and emphasizing differing levels of legibility. "TYPE CAN TAKE A BACK SEAT, OR IT CAN SHOUT LOUD AND DEMAND TO BE NOTICED. WHICHEVER VIEW IS TAKEN, LEGIBILITY IS KEY," says Graham Vickers.

156

LAYOUT:
MAKING IT FIT

In place of a catalog, Philip Fass produced this eight-page barrel-fold brochure for Joyce Scott's exhibition at the University of Northern Iowa Gallery of Art. Fass's design provides the reader with a real experience of the detail, color, and texture of Scott's work by typographically representing its thousands of glass beads in his interpretation of the artist's statement. The extensive resume then makes use of fine, condensed san serif letterforms in order to accommodate the quantity of information, as well as visually complement the more decorative elements.

DESIGN FIRM **PHILIP FASS** ● DESIGN
PHILIP FASS ● CLIENT **UNIVERSITY
OF NORTHERN IOWA GALLERY OF ART**
● PROJECT NAME **JOYCE SCOTT
INVITATION**

By introducing transparent, ochre halftones on all the pages relating to this article in **Dwell**, the designer has provided a visual element that not only gives further information, but also allows type and image to overlap without detriment to legibility or sense. Designers created dynamic thumbnails, which allowed them the space to run full-bleed images and give the content more visual variety and movement. The overall design concept is strong, with excellent color coordination, interesting typographic relationships, and contrasts of scale and rhythm, with the inclusion of these more unusual elements being both spatially practical and visually attractive.

At left, the view from the front door shows how Wintersole's design makes the most of the house's 950 square feet. The furniture helps, too. As Mike explains, "These pieces don't consume visual space." Above, a rather precarious catwalk leads to the bedroom. Mike designed the entertainment center (below) with components from Elfa.

Story by Allison Arieff | Photos by Scogin Mayo

Which House Costs $120,000?

Answer: They both do. Here's how one young couple who refused to buy into the developer version of a dream home built one of their very own.

Project: LaBry & Young Residence
Architect: Richard Wintersole
Location: Burleson, Texas

56 Dwell October 2002

In the Dallas/Fort Worth Metroplex, there is no shortage of three-bedroom, two-car-garage homes for sale on newly created streets with names like Running Brook Drive and Brittany Place. It's almost a given that young couples in search of their first home go straight to developments by companies like Centex, Dissmore, History Maker Homes, or any one of the many builders in the area. These homes are all spacious, well appointed, and reasonably priced, to be sure—but each seems nearly indistinguishable from the next.

"People don't want to make choices or take chances," Gayla LaBry observes. "That's why they buy those developer homes."

Gayla and her husband, Michael Young, who describes himself to me as "a strong, aggressive personality" (as Gayla nods her head vigorously in agreement), wanted something different. "I think outside the box," says Mike who works as a project engineer for Acme Brick in Fort Worth. "You see that at work and in the way our home turned out."

Mike and Gayla, who works in finance, met during college in Lafayette, Louisiana, and in 1996, after a year in Germany, moved to Fort Worth. In a town where football and church are the primary cultural activities, this couple has made more treks through Europe than PBS' Rick Steves. When they accumulated $1,000 worth of books and magazines to research ideas for their new home, the stack included not only *Southern Living* but *Abitare* and *Domus*. And while their peers were happily handing over down payments for 3,000 square feet of brass-fixtured, shag-carpeted colonials, Mike and Gayla presented an architect with their idea of a dream home, hired him, and paid for the whole thing in cash.

When they made the decision to build rather than buy, Mike and Gayla chose a lot in Burleson, about 20 minutes south of Fort Worth. In contrast to the brick-veneered homes in the unabated sprawl of "affordable luxury" housing developments clustered off I-35, their little neighborhood is a refreshing pocket of individuality. "I wish I'd been born here," says Gayla. "I feel like I was." The houses in this working-class community are unremarkable but unique. As you turn off the main drag just past Wal-Mart, there's a newly minted colonial, a '70s-era bunker with grass growing on the roof, and a modest ranch house featuring an artful if puzzling pattern of undulating bricks. It's a libertarian's dream here—people just let each other be. So when the couple began work on their 950-square-foot house-as-loft project on Pecan Drive, the only thing anyone asked was, "You're not putting a trailer on the lot, are you?"

Mike was working at that time for a glass company, where he had supervised the construction of a steel-frame addition to the factory. He was fascinated by the technique, and for a variety of reasons ranging from aesthetics to termite-resistance, he was intent on using a steel frame for his own house. All he needed was an architect. ▶

October 2002 **Dwell** 59

DESIGN FIRM **DWELL MAGAZINE**
PRODUCTION ● ART DIRECTION
JEANETTE ABBINK ● DESIGN **SHAUN**
HAZEN ● CLIENT *DWELL* **MAGAZINE**
● PROJECT NAME *DWELL*, **"WHICH**
HOUSE COSTS $120,000?"

Dwellings

Details, shown clockwise from the top left corner: ground-floor window detail, exposed ducts, a plywood bridge that connects the staircase to the bedroom, sandblasted steel railings, exterior Galvalume siding, frosted glass panels for privacy, industrial diamond-plate stairs, shelving system by Elfa, and in the center, view of the side entrance.

Steel Frames

Architects like Richard Neutra, Albert Frey, Pierre Koenig, and the Eameses may have all designed houses with it, but, historically, steel framing has held a small market share among single-family homes built in the United States. However for a variety of reasons—most notably the rising cost (and dwindling supply) of lumber and the stable price of steel—this type of fabrication is gaining popularity in the world of residential architecture.

Why? Steel possesses the highest strength-to-weight ratio of any building material utilized today, and is one of the strongest, most durable, and economically manufactured materials available. It doesn't rot, warp, or split. It makes for straighter walls and less cracking in drywall and plaster. It's both fire-resistant and termite-proof. Steel framing produces less waste on the job site. And it's lightweight, making it easier to handle than wood frames.

For the Young/LaBry residence, Classic Steel Frame Homes adapted one of their standardized systems, usually used for conventional models, and fabricated a steel frame based on architect Rick Wintersole's working drawings. The red iron frame (above), which was bolted rather than welded together, supports the roof and floors of the house; galvanized metal studs fill in the spaces between. The benefits of this building system quickly became apparent to Rick, and since completing the steel-frame house in 2000, he has built two more.

"I really love the aesthetic of steel," Rick explains. "I can't understand why people want to cover it up. It's like taking a lie. You have this wonderful thing and then you cover it. Being able to see the steel or any other building material, you're telling the story of how the house was built." —A.A.

The Fort Worth AIA put the adventurous couple in touch with architect Richard Wintersole. It was a perfect match, and since Rick's idea of marketing himself is "sitting by the phone and waiting for it to ring," the Young/LaBry commission came as a pleasant surprise.

Architecture is a second career for the mild-mannered and wry-humored Texan, who was originally trained as a microbiologist. The determination and resolve that comes with starting out in a new field later in life has no doubt aided his efforts to work in a modernist vernacular in a community reared to desire gabled roofs. His own home in the suburb of Aledo, Texas, which he shares with wife, Margaret, a journalist, and son Colin, 17, is an elegant corrugated-metal-and-glass structure with a barrel-vaulted ceiling that takes its inspiration from Louis Kahn's Kimbell Art Museum. "We're probably considered to be communists or something out where we are," says Rick, who is just completing construction on a house for a client in Keller, Texas, that has industrial stairs and a camouflage roof. "Margaret has to hide her subscription to *Mother Jones*."

Mike and Gayla were clear about what they wanted—something clean, modern, and minimalist—and knew what they could afford. "We wanted something unique," says Mike. "We didn't want to copy someone's design, but we also weren't interested in something so different that it didn't look right." At $120,000, the budget was small, but because the site was located in an unincorporated part of town, the codes and restrictions that normally dictate home construction were not in place, so Rick knew he could have more freedom with his design.

Mike enthusiastically marketed the steel-frame option to Rick, who at first wasn't convinced. "I don't think the day that I sat down with a blank piece of paper I was thinking it was going to be a metal building," he explains. But when contractors' bids started coming in, the steel-framing turned out to be not only the clients' preference but also the most cost-effective option.

Rick's initial reticence had been based on his prior experience with steel companies. "When I'd dealt with them before," he explains, "they basically just wanted to sell steel. The closest thing these companies have to an architect is the guy who does the CAD work for them. And once the house is complete, it's like you're not supposed to know that it's steel anymore. It's supposed to look like everybody else's house."

Houston's Classic Steel Frame Homes was willing to transform Rick's working drawings into a steel frame for the house, though the company—which manufactures a line of Tudorish homes with names like the Palace and the Oxford 10Plex—wondered why the client didn't want to just pick an existing design from their brochure. Once the fabrication was complete, the company loaded up everything from the floor joists to the roof purlins, trucked it from Houston to Burleson, and laid it out in the yard like an outsize set of Tinkertoys. The frame ▶

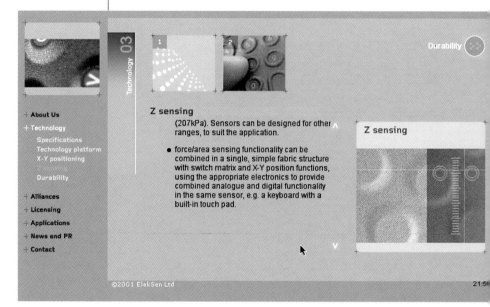

Z sensing

(207kPa). Sensors can be designed for other ranges, to suit the application.

- force/area sensing functionality can be combined in a single, simple fabric structure with switch matrix and X-Y position functions, using the appropriate electronics to provide combined analogue and digital functionality in the same sensor, e.g. a keyboard with a built-in touch pad.

©2001 ElekSen Ltd

DESIGN FIRM **HOLLER** ● DESIGN
WILL PYNE ● CLIENT **ELEKSEN** ●
PROJECT NAME **ELEKSEN WEB SITE,**
WWW.ELEKSEN.CO.UK

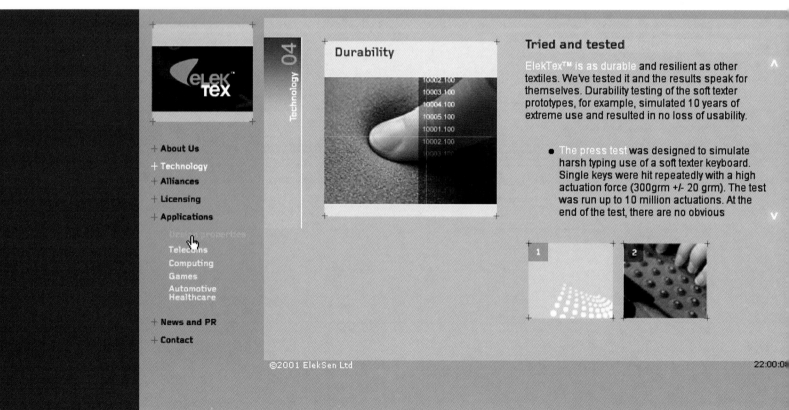

Durability

Tried and tested

ElekTex™ is as durable and resilient as other textiles. We've tested it and the results speak for themselves. Durability testing of the soft texter prototypes, for example, simulated 10 years of extreme use and resulted in no loss of usability.

- The press test was designed to simulate harsh typing use of a soft texter keyboard. Single keys were hit repeatedly with a high actuation force (300grm +/- 20 grm). The test was run up to 10 million actuations. At the end of the test, there are no obvious

©2001 ElekSen Ltd

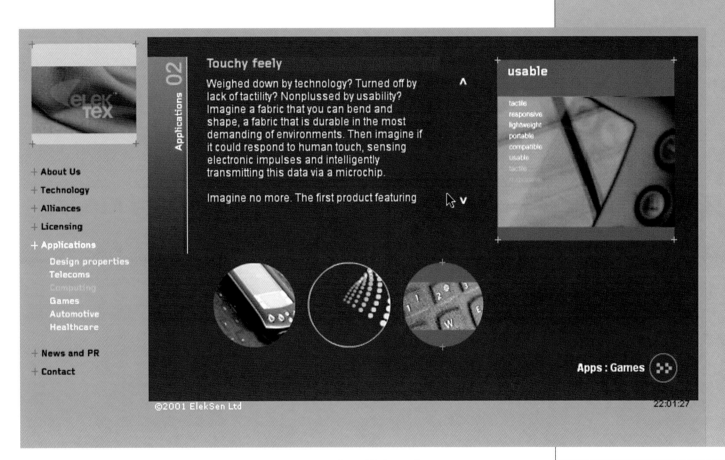

Web sites are notoriously difficult to read when a lot of information has to be conveyed to the viewer. "ONE OF THE MOST CHALLENGING ASPECTS OF THE ELEKSEN SITE," says James Kirkham of Holler, "WAS TO INCLUDE ALL THE MAIN COPY SUPPLIED BY THE CLIENT." The designers have skillfully broken down the text into different levels and treatments, combining it with evolving images and animated diagrams to make reading easy and enjoyable. On every page, colors, shapes, textures, and tones help to create meaningful layouts. One of the most successful design devices that the designers used to accommodate the considerable text is a scrolling process comprising two unobtrusive arrows. This allows the viewer to access written information in manageable, coherent "bites" rather than needing to progress through different pages or tackle large quantities of copy in one go.

161

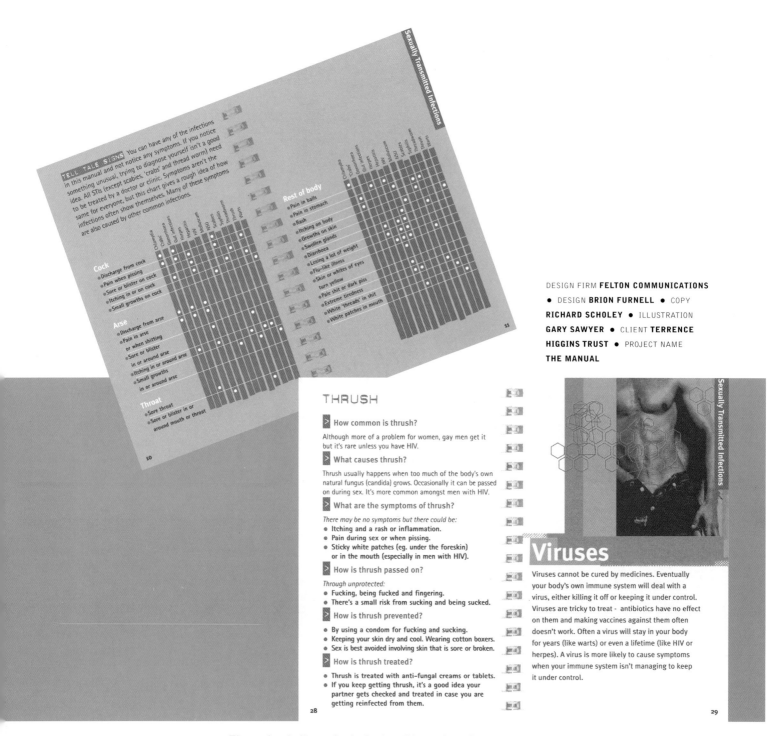

TELL TALE SIGNS You can have any of the infections in this manual and not notice any symptoms. If you notice something unusual, trying to diagnose yourself isn't a good idea. All STIs (except scabies, 'crabs' and thread worm) need to be treated by a doctor or clinic. Symptoms aren't the same for everyone, but this chart gives a rough idea of how infections often show themselves. Many of these symptoms are also caused by other common infections.

Cock
- Discharge from cock
- Pain when pissing
- Sore or blister on cock
- Itching in or on cock
- Small growths on cock

Arse
- Discharge from arse
- Pain in arse or when shitting
- Sore or blister in or around arse
- Itching in or around arse
- Small growths in or around arse

Throat
- Sore throat
- Sore or blister in or around mouth or throat

Rest of body
- Pain in balls
- Pain in stomach
- Rash
- Itching on body
- Growths on skin
- Swollen glands
- Diarrhoea
- Losing a lot of weight
- Flu-like illness
- Skin or whites of eyes turn yellow
- Pale shit or dark piss
- Extreme tiredness
- White 'threads' in shit
- White patches in mouth

10   11

DESIGN FIRM **FELTON COMMUNICATIONS**
● DESIGN **BRION FURNELL** ● COPY
RICHARD SCHOLEY ● ILLUSTRATION
GARY SAWYER ● CLIENT **TERRENCE
HIGGINS TRUST** ● PROJECT NAME
THE MANUAL

THRUSH

> **How common is thrush?**

Although more of a problem for women, gay men get it but it's rare unless you have HIV.

> **What causes thrush?**

Thrush usually happens when too much of the body's own natural fungus (candida) grows. Occasionally it can be passed on during sex. It's more common amongst men with HIV.

> **What are the symptoms of thrush?**

There may be no symptoms but there could be:
- Itching and a rash or inflammation.
- Pain during sex or when pissing.
- Sticky white patches (eg. under the foreskin) or in the mouth (especially in men with HIV).

> **How is thrush passed on?**

Through unprotected:
- Fucking, being fucked and fingering.
- There's a small risk from sucking and being sucked.

> **How is thrush prevented?**

- By using a condom for fucking and sucking.
- Keeping your skin dry and cool. Wearing cotton boxers.
- Sex is best avoided involving skin that is sore or broken.

> **How is thrush treated?**

- Thrush is treated with anti-fungal creams or tablets.
- If you keep getting thrush, it's a good idea your partner gets checked and treated in case you are getting reinfected from them.

28

Viruses

Viruses cannot be cured by medicines. Eventually your body's own immune system will deal with a virus, either killing it off or keeping it under control. Viruses are tricky to treat - antibiotics have no effect on them and making vaccines against them often doesn't work. Often a virus will stay in your body for years (like warts) or even a lifetime (like HIV or herpes). A virus is more likely to cause symptoms when your immune system isn't managing to keep it under control.

29

The main challenge in designing this pocket-sized manual was to present all the information in a logical yet attractive manner that is easy to digest.

Inevitably, there is insufficient space to create visual interest through varieties of scale and composition, so typographic changes in color and weight are used, and an intriguing printed version of a metal spiral binding runs down the spine on each spread. Where possible, small illustrations break up the text, and diagrammatic interpretations substitute wordy passages. Attention to detailing can be seen, for example, in the uneven column lengths of the charts on the orange pages, making this piece both visually pleasing and practical.

These two single pages are part of a bound-in supplement on new furniture and architectural design. They bring together an eclectic mix of products in visually exciting layouts without compromising the clear presentation of information. Blocks of color, text, and photography fill the pages and are geometrically montaged together with sensitive consideration for asymmetric balance and rhythm. The mixing of ranged left and right type in both vertical and horizontal orientations not only increases the visible vitality but also encourages a viewer's engagement with the topics.

DESIGN FIRM **EXQUISITE CORPORATION** ● ART DIRECTION **RILEY JOHN-DONNELL** ● DESIGN **RILEY JOHN-DONNELL** ● COPY **JEREMY LIN** ● CLIENT *SURFACE* **MAGAZINE** ● PROJECT NAME *SURFACE*

promise of a new level of intimacy between viewer and viewed, between art and experience.

SFMOMA has been at the forefront of multimedia development since 1993, when the Museum began producing award-winning interactive projects such as the *Voices and Images of California Art* CD-ROM and the 1999 *Bill Viola* Web site feature (http://www.sfmoma.org/exhibitions/viola/index.html) to help illuminate artists and their work. Now, with *Making Sense of Modern Art*, the Museum brings context back to the artwork for the eyes and ears of individual visitors. Covering the major artists, works, and movements represented in SFMOMA's collection, the new digital project spans the history of twentieth-century art. When the program is complete, expert commentary by renowned artists, curators, critics, and art historians will illuminate more than one hundred pieces in all media—from paintings, sculpture, and photography to media arts, architecture, and design—with a special emphasis on works in SFMOMA's permanent collection. The resulting multimedia experience will be an educational journey for everyone, from novice museumgoers to avid art historians.

What is art without context? "So much is missing when a person views a work of art in a gallery," notes Peter Samis,

SFMOMA associate curator of education and program manager for interactive educational technologies. "So much has been stripped away—the artist isn't there, the studio isn't there, the time in which the piece was created is most likely long gone. All these elements, however, bring an important context to the work.

"It's difficult not to notice that when many people—members of the general public—come into a museum, they end up reporting in frustration that they saw, for example, 'just a pile of stones,' while an artist or art historian can enter the same room, let his or her gaze linger over the same stones, and see in them a poetic, touching commentary on the continued, if threatened, survival of nature within culture. The artist and art historian have the advantage of context. It's as if a hundred associations, things seen, things known, and things only dimly intuited have come together in a flash, sending synapses firing in a flare of recognition and excitement."

Samis believes that we glean meaning through relationships—through involving ourselves in a network of references. His goal, and that of project manager Susie

Wise and other talented team members, is thus to create a tool to help people recognize and comprehend these myriad connections. The result: *Making Sense of Modern Art*.

Three interfaces for experiential learning

Making Sense of Modern Art, which will be available in April 2000 at multimedia learning stations within the Museum's galleries and in partial form on SFMOMA's Web site, offers visitors three complementary approaches to understanding art. All of the approaches foster inquiry; each propels visitors to move beyond merely glancing at the dates and facts presented on wall labels and invites them, instead, to enter into the spirit of the work. The interfaces correspond with three different ways of seeing: examining an individual work, comparing it to others, and exploring themes across time.

If you were to click on Robert Rauschenberg's 1954 painting *Collection (Formerly Untitled)* through the individual artwork interface, you could explore answers to frequently asked questions about the painting; zoom in on a particular brushstroke or collage fragment, pictured in life size; and see and hear archival film and video excerpts showing Rauschenberg speaking about his work. You could

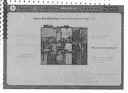

Lisa Schiffman, the author of Generation J (Harper San Francisco), works as an Internet strategist for major corporations.

Major support for Making Sense of Modern Art is provided by The Getty Grant Program and Compaq Computer Corporation. Additional support is provided by the Consulate General of Switzerland, San Francisco.

access interviews with other artists, well-known critics, historians, and collectors, and you could find out what critics had to say about a work the first time it was exhibited. You could listen to music or read extracts from poetry and explore documentary photographs related to the painting or its creation.

Perhaps you decide, instead, to choose the comparative approach, creating instant dialogues between the many artworks arrayed on the introductory timeline. You click and drag one work to another; say, perhaps, you pull the Rauschenberg painting on top of Henri Matisse's *Femme au chapeau* (Woman with a Hat) to learn from the resulting juxtapositions. Works that may not have been created in the same country or during the same time period now find themselves in a comparative relationship, offering surprising and revelatory analogies. At a conceptual level, this

interface mimics the classic dual slide projector method of instruction, which is used in traditional art history classes to examine similarities and differences between works of art. But at an experiential level, *Making Sense of Modern Art* takes the idea a step further, giving the student, not the teacher, the power of choice.

The third approach, themes across time, offers the unique opportunity to explore single or multiple questions across an entire century. If you click on a question such as "Who gave modern artists the right to make their own rules?" you might find yourself transported through a set of screens reaching back to the nineteenth century and forward to the present, including artists, collectors, curators, and critics as diverse as Gustave Courbet and Jeff Koons, Lillie Bliss and Kiki Smith. The ensuing series of mini-narratives eventually form a many-layered whole, a

story that ties together a stream of work spanning modernity.

The result of these three interfaces, bundled into one interactive program, is a powerful tool for highlighting the unique properties inherent in each artwork, helping us to make connections across space and time, and, ultimately, teaching us how to ask questions and draw our own conclusions about art.

According to Samis, "When people are stopped in their tracks by an artwork, in that pause, they might find a thread in that void between the words, a germ of a new idea that they want to pursue." This is the aim, then, of *Making Sense of Modern Art*: to stop people in their tracks. Not for seven seconds or even ten, but for however long it takes for the spark of discovery to light and then burn or for the artwork before them to become something more than simply an object hanging on a wall. ▣

DESIGN FIRM **APPETITE ENGINEERS** ● ART DIRECTION **KEIKO HAYASHI (SFMOMA)** ● DESIGN **MARTIN VENEZKY** ● CLIENT **SAN FRANCISCO MUSEUM OF MODERN ART** ● PROJECT NAME ***OPEN***

38 open

39 open

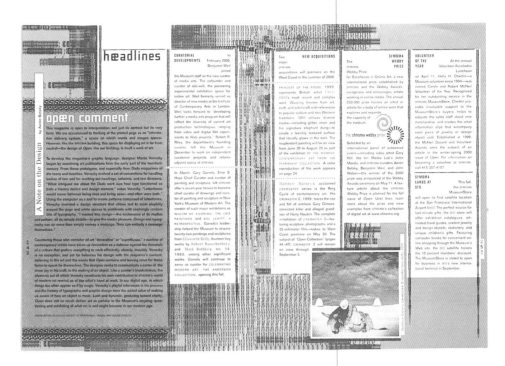

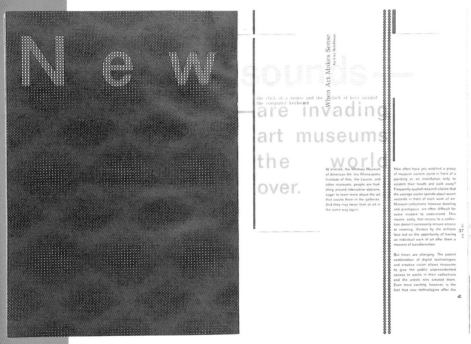

These layouts from *Open*, the magazine for members of the San Francisco Museum of Modern Art, display a distinct sense of building, of evolving. Text and imagery construct the pages in an organic way. Color, texture, and tone, whether created by type or imagery, come together to produce individual compositions that are as much about abstract style as they are about imparting hard information.

Martin Venezky says that he wanted the design of *Open,* with the "EXUBERANCE OF ITS RHYTHM AND PATTERN, AND ALL ITS MINUTE DETAILS" to give the reader pleasure. Venezky continues, "DESIGN AND TYPOGRAPHY CAN DO MORE THAN SIMPLY CONVEY A MESSAGE—THEY CAN EMBODY A MESSAGE THEMSELVES."

DESIGN FIRM **GREENFIELD/BELSER LTD.** ● ART DIRECTION **BURKEY BELSER** ● DESIGN **LISA CORBETT, CHARLYNE FABI** ● COPY **LISE ANNE SCHWARTZ** ● CLIENT **PILSBURY WINTHROP** ● PROJECT NAME **RECRUITING BROCHURE**

Keen competition by U.S. law firms for new graduate talent is what encouraged Greenfield/Belser to conceive this unusual format for Pilsbury Winthrop's recruitment brochure.
The information is broken down into "bite-size" chunks that are shown on fifteen individual pages, collated into a swatch. Each colorful section offers helpful advice to potential recruits. Both questions and answers are contained within the small, slim format, making this wealth of information extremely easy to navigate.

DESIGN FIRM **GEE + CHUNG** ● ART DIRECTION **EARL GEE** ● DESIGN **EARL GEE, FANI CHUNG** ● COPY **JAMIE MARKS** ● PHOTOGRAPHY **KEVIN IRBY** ● CLIENT **XINET, INC.** ● PROJECT NAME **XINET BROCHURE**

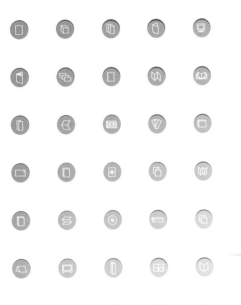

Expanding your business: now and in the future. Different industries discover product benefits in different ways.

FULLPRESS, WEBNATIVE & WEBNATIVE VENTURE: INNOVATIVE SOLUTIONS FOR COMPETITIVE MARKETS

XINET'S SCALABLE SOLUTIONS GROW WITH YOUR BUSINESS, SPEEDING LOCAL AND REMOTE PRODUCTION ACROSS THE OFFICE AND AROUND THE WORLD.

FullPress® server software alleviates the bottlenecks that businesses encounter when they work with large image files. With FullPress at the center of the workflow, managing file-sharing, minimizing network traffic, and sending output to any device on the network, sites can speed production, reduce costs and increase output.

Adding *WebNative*™ to the FullPress workflow extends services over the Internet, giving customers, staff and collaborative partners instant access to digital assets. In addition to the advantages of centralized multi-site asset sharing, WebNative also streamlines many production activities, such as re-purposing, proofing,

archiving and restoring. WebNative is an incredibly versatile system that can be used for corporate brand management, as well as creating new Web-enabled production workflows.

Xinet's *WebNative*™ *Venture* combines all of the functionality and ease-of-use of WebNative with an enterprise-strength SQL database—for even faster searching, organizing, and categorizing of data—creating an asset-management system that's completely and automatically integrated into each site's existing FullPress workflow.

FULLPRESS: REMOVING WORKFLOW BOTTLENECKS

FULLPRESS PROVIDES FAST FILE SHARING, ADVANCED IMAGE REPLACEMENT TECHNOLOGY, PRINT SPOOLING, AND TOOLS WHICH SOLVE THE PROBLEMS SITES FACE DURING PRODUCTION.

Centralized file services
FullPress stores shared files in volumes on the central server. Mac users select volumes through the *Chooser* and they appear on their desktops. Files in these mounted FullPress volumes can be manipulated just as if they were on the user's local disk.

Xinet's file-sharing technology is unique because FullPress can present users with many views of a single high-resolution file. This improves efficiency because it allows people to work with the same file simultaneously, in several different ways.

FullPress technology: one file, many views
When high-res images are placed or scanned onto the FullPress server, FullPress automatically generates low-res views of these files and presents them in a corresponding FPO ("For Placement Only") volume. As photo retouchers edit the original high-res files, they work from the "High Res" volume. At the same time, designers use the corresponding low-res FPO versions in layouts, working from the "FPO" volume. FullPress also makes it possible for users to log in over the Internet with Xinet's WebNative software and view the same file as a GIF or JPEG, in a "Web" image volume.

Although these volumes appear to contain separate files, behind the scenes, FullPress is actually presenting users with different "windows" into the exact same high-res original. Xinet technology ensures that any changes made to a high-resolution image are instantly apparent in all of its corresponding views.

Seamless substitution upon output
When operators print files to a FullPress print-spooler, FullPress replaces FPO views with high-resolution images and applies any modifications that have been set within the layout application—just as if operators had been working with the high-res data all along. Print jobs clear workstations in seconds and arrive at output devices very quickly!

FullPress supports the most file formats
FullPress supports over 20 image file formats, making it the most versatile server software in the industry. Images in any of these filetypes can be placed on the FullPress server and incorporated directly into programs such as QuarkXPress® and Illustrator® without additional work. There's no need to flatten layers or convert proprietary file formats. This saves time, and makes it easy for you to use images from almost any system inside your FullPress workflow.

SUPPORTED IMAGE FILE FORMATS
- Alias PIX
- BARCO CT
- BARCO LW
- BMP
- Contex CT
- Crosfield Studio 9000 (Crosfield DDEF)
- DALIM CT (with masks)
- DALIM LW
- DCS 1.0 and 2.0
- Eclipse TILE
- EPS/EPSF (else JPEG-encoded)
- Erkafort/EskoScan
- JPEG (JFIF)
- Kodak PhotoDisk
- PDF
- Photoshop native
- Scitex CT (alias MaxileCutter)
- Scitex LW
- SGI RGB (SGI image Library)
- Sun raster file
- TIFF (including masks and spot colors)
- TIFF/IT P1
- X Window dump
- Image file formats are added frequently; contact Xinet for the latest list.

"Without a stable prepress department, it's impossible for a printing business to grow. Since we implemented the Xinet workflow, our annual revenue has doubled."

CARLSON WESTH
city Tech Manager
Champaign Fine Printing
Champaign part of
the Red Wild Fort Group
Houston Texas

"Le Courrier de l'Ouest uses FullPress to produce the newspaper's advertising and editorial sections, spending up several stages of production. Now, we meet all of our deadlines easily."

CHRISTOPHE PERON
Production Information Engineer
Le Courrier de l'Ouest, a daily newspaper with a circulation of 115,000 that produces eight full-color editions for different readership areas
Angers, France

In the opening to this section, we discussed iconic substitution. In this brochure for Xinet, Inc., Gee + Chung has originated a multitude of simple icons that symbolize many varied industries. Instead of simply viewing a list, the reader, is invited to interact with the brochure's paper engineering pullout, which quickly reveals a far more extensive set of icons than had first been viewed. Contrasting with this unexpected pneumonic device, the second section of the brochure continues to present quantities of information. This time it is of a more technical nature, with copy and diagrams positioned within a visible grid, helping to accommodate and structure the considerable data.

167

The appetizers section is a regular inclusion in *Waitrose Food Illustrated* magazine. Made up of articles by a number of writers, the pace and rhythm of this section as a whole is varied and unpredictable. The "Fresh Ideas" page from the July 2002 issue brings together five separate, small articles, each functioning within its own individual grouping, but also operating as part of the complete page. This is successfully achieved by making use of every available space, a strong grid system, consistent spatial relationships, and careful regard for alignments.

DESIGN FIRM **JOHN BROWN CITRUS PUBLISHING** ● ART DIRECTION **DANIEL BIASATTI** ● DESIGN **SONA HART** ● CLIENT **WAITROSE FOOD ILLUSTRATED** MAGAZINE ● PROJECT NAME **WAITROSE FOOD ILLUSTRATED, "APPETISERS: FRESH IDEAS"**

NOT TO BE TRIFLED WITH
Make your summer salads extra special with a dressing made from El Majuelo Macetilla Sherry Vinegar (£3.95/250ml) and heady extra virgin olive oil. This vinegar, which is exclusive to Waitrose, is made to an ancient recipe, using a special fermentation process that has its roots in 14th century Andalusia. After fermentation, El Majuelo Macetilla Sherry Vinegar is aged in oak barrels for several years, allowing it to develop a milder aroma and sweeter taste than most sherry vinegars on the market. This sweetness and the lack of bitter aftertaste make it perfect for sprinkling over fresh strawberries to create an instant summer dessert, as well as for use in casseroles or with game.

JULY is a good month to...

Fresh ideas

Keep things simple this month, with hunks of Spanish cheese, delicious pasta sauces and some unusual vinegar

APPETISERS

PARTY ONLINE
Plan your summer's entertaining at www.waitrose.com/barbecue. There are more than 100 food and cocktail recipes to help you create a truly wonderful spread. You can even use the online invites to let everybody know about the party. And to make life even easier, order your wine online and have it delivered to your door. For more details, visit www.waitrose.com.

LA MANCHA MUNCH
Spain's best-known and best-loved cheese, Manchego is made from sheep's milk in La Mancha, an area in the heart of the country. A crumbly textured, pale-coloured cheese (£11.49/kg) with a nutty, buttery taste, Manchego is good on its own, but is best with *membrillo* (£1.89/240g), a quince paste that is its classic accompaniment. Quince is a yellow fruit, that's very acidic raw, but turns into a rich, ruby jelly when cooked with sugar. A scoop of *membrillo* on a chunk of Manchego is a wonderful way to end a meal, or to have as a snack with a drink. Why not stay with the Spanish theme and enjoy it with a glass of fruity Rioja?

PASTA RESISTANCE
The new Bistro line of fresh pasta sauces at Waitrose are perfect for creating tasty meals in a trice. Made from the highest quality ingredients, these sauces allow you to make easy suppers that are packed with authentic flavours. Using fresh tomatoes, fresh herbs, extra virgin olive oil and, for the creamy sauces, proper roux and flavour-infused milk, Bistro pasta sauces are prepared so that they keep as much of the taste and colour of their ingredients as possible – and that includes cooking the vegetables separately. Among the delicious flavours available in the Bistro line are Tomato, Mozzarella and Rocket, *above, served with fusilli lungi*, (£2.39/350g), Salmon and Asparagus (£2.49/350g) and Mediterranean Vegetable (£2.29/350g).

● Gallop down to Goodwood and have a flutter on the gee-gees. The Chichester racecourse celebrates its 200th birthday this year, and the Glorious Goodwood meeting (30 July–3 August) is the centrepiece. For more information on this and other commemorative events, log on to www.goodwood.co.uk.
● Find the perfect cottage hideaway. Thatched rooves, four-posters, open fires, dreamy gardens… whatever you desire, the *Good Holiday Cottage Guide 2002* (Swallow Press, £5.95) will help you to find that beautiful bolthole.
● Develop a way with words at the Dartington Hall Festival, 12–21 July, in deepest Devon. A jam-packed programme gives book-lovers the chance to meet writers including Fay Weldon, Pat Barker, Mo Mowlam and Alain de Botton. Contact Ways with Words on 01803 867373, or visit www.wayswithwords.co.uk.
● Prepare yourself for the summer holidays by reading Rohan Candappa's *Parent's Survival Handbook* (Ebury, £3.99), a hilarious spin on the self-help genre, which includes crucial advice, such as: "before feeding chocolate to a small child, smear some over your own clothes. It saves time."

32

DESIGN FIRM **[I]E DESIGN** • ART
DIRECTION **MARCIE CARSON** •
DESIGN **CYA NELSON** • CLIENT
LEGEND AUDIO • PROJECT NAME
ART OF SOUND BROCHURE

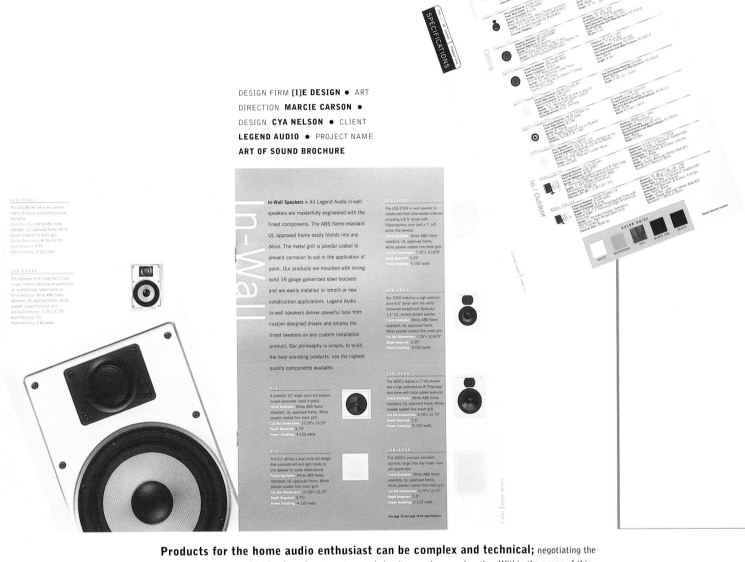

Products for the home audio enthusiast can be complex and technical; negotiating the
multitude of woofers, tweeters, and circuitry can be very daunting. Within the pages of this
Legend Audio Art of Sound brochure, [i]e Design has successfully made a wealth of technical
information inviting and accessible. Making exciting use of a fifth color metallic ink, juxtaposed
cut-out imagery, and diverse typographic texture and tone, Cya Nelson and Marcie Carson filled
the pages of this brochure with stylish product information. Creating dynamic contrast with
opposite pages, some spreads contain the majority of text within half of their space, while loading
the specific product detailing into a multipage directory at the end of the brochure.

Paradise Lost?

WITH THE KUTA BOMB SURF CULTURE CHANGED FOREVER. THE 'WAR ON TERROR' IS NO LONGER ESCAPABLE SIMPLY BY LIGHTING UP, PADDLING OUT AND FORGETTING ABOUT IT. THE FRONTIERS OF SURF HEDONISM HAVE BECOME THE FRONT LINES.

By **DC GREEN** Illustrated by **ROSS HOLDEN**

On most of my Indo jaunts, the most radical thing I usually write about is which pro surfer lost his eyebrow in which drunken bout of flatday boat fun. But this - the gutless slaughter of revellers from around the world by a hulking fertiliser bomb planted in a road-blocking bemo outside two popular Kuta night clubs - is different. It's the heaviest and perhaps the most significant watershed in surfing history.

We surfers were, after all, the harbingers of capitalism, nightclubs, mega-tourism and all that Bali has become today. All, in other words, the terrorists despise. On this island of spirits, I feel an almost crushing responsibility to write something that will pay sufficient tribute to the multitude of people from many nations (including two young surfers from my home town on their first overseas trip) who were murdered in the Sari Club and Paddy's on October 12, and the hundreds more who will carry horrendous physical and psychological scars to their graves.

Of the hundred-odd surf magazines and net sites scattered around the globe, I was the only surf journalist to go to Bali: a damning indictment of my junket-sniffing brethren. Yet, soon after I landed - into a climate of paralysing heat and sadness, just days after - I began to feel massively inadequate. I wanted to run away and go surfing somewhere and leave the coverage to the hundreds of 'real' journalists. Then I noticed how these so-called professionals swarm around more like a collective individual; all bunkered and buffered together in the luxurious Hard Rock Hotel; all sitting together in the same press conferences (also conveniently held at the Hard Rock); all taking the same notes and photos; and all even flying out together 11 days after the bomb, almost to a man. I began to feel better - still depressed but less insecure. Yet I knew,

IRAQ: DEMON DESPOTS AND THE PAPER TIGERS

Hussein would be crazy to fund terrorism outside 'Iraq because any bomb that could be traced back to Baghdad would be the perfect excuse for Bush to kick-start Desert Storm TWO. So he contents himself with torturing his own people. Yes, Hussein is a mass murdering despot who deserves to be ousted - the problem is, so do half the other regimes in the world. Perhaps Hussein has stock-piled weapons of mass destruction and defied UN resolutions - the problem is, so has Israel. That

THE USA: GUARDIANS OF FREEDOM OR AGENTS PROVOCATEURS?

"What difference does it make to the dead, the orphans and the homeless, whether the mad destruction is wrought under the name of totalitarianism or the holy name of liberty or democracy?" Mahatma Gandhi (1869 - 1948)

When the giant mushroom cloud rose over Kuta on October 12, Made Switra (whose shop

equally, we can assume, loathed by bin Laden. America seems oblivious to this inherent hypocrisy is what riles the Arab Muslim world so much. Oh yes, and did someone mention oil?

AL QAEDA: COHERENT NETWORK OR CONJURED DEMON?

Four weeks after the attack, al Qaeda claimed responsibility for the bomb on a website. Even

DESIGN FIRM **MEDIA CELL, LTD.** ●
DESIGN **MICKEY BOY G** ● COPY **D C
GREEN** ● ILLUSTRATION **ROSS
HOLDEN** ● CLIENT **ADRENALIN
MAGAZINE** ● PROJECT NAME
ADRENALIN

170

Red and white has to be an appropriate option for an editorial on the Bali atrocity in 2002. The way it has been used, however, has the effect of deceiving the readers, as they are initially only aware of the black type on white, and the red shapes appear as graphic imagery. Changes in pace and degrees of difficulty tend to make the reading experience more participatory. Moving from black on white to black on red, as well as through differing point sizes and weights, makes the process harder, and in some ways reminiscent of the noisy, crowded environment of Kuta in Bali, which was clearly exacerbated by the bombing. It is also interesting to recognize the semiotic language created by this use of red, as it flows over and around the text, like spilt blood. The illustrations are clearly deliberately "lightweight" despite being visually intriguing, in order to allow the areas of red to dominate.

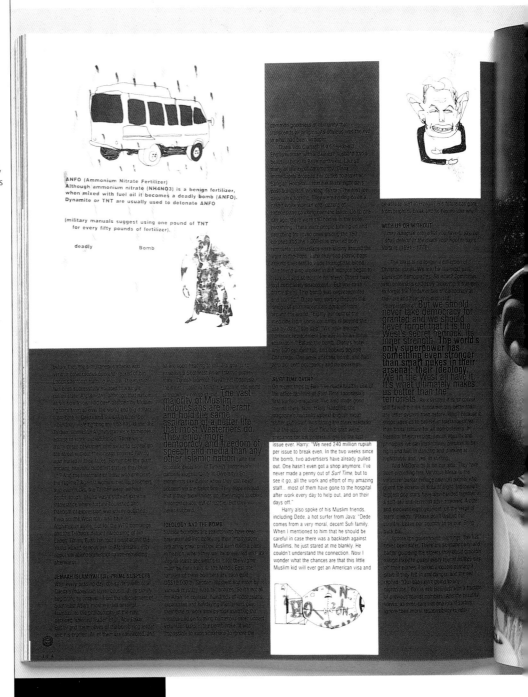

ANFO (Ammonium Nitrate Fertilizer)
Although ammonium nitrate (NH4NO3) is a benign fertilizer, when mixed with fuel oil it becomes a deadly bomb (ANFO). Dynamite or TNT are usually used to detonate ANFO.

(military manuals suggest using one pound of TNT for every fifty pounds of fertilizer).

deadly   Bomb

Altered perception

The art of printing

Things are not what they seem. In this trio of articles, what you thought of as black and white will be completely changed. Open your mind to the monochrome.

For a tiny number of people, the world is devoid of colour – not always a handicap, as GRAHAM VICKERS reports (below).

When printing even the simplest photograph, the process you choose can drastically change the image's effect, says KRISTOFFER ALBRECHT (opposite)

And even black isn't simply dark ink. Each different printing method reveals an explosion of colour in the work of ground-breaking artist ADAM LOWE (page 13)

Behind all of its many connotations lies the physical reality of black and white – pure white being defined as fully reflected light, pure black being the near or total absorption of light. In fact these absolute opposites are rather less clear-cut than one might think, as a huge amount depends on the perception of the viewer and its context. After all, a grey square can appear nearly white against dark surroundings – or as washed-out black if placed against a white background. Similarly, pure black can only be perceived as such if its surface is smooth and glossy, since a matt finish introduces fine surface irregularities which themselves reflect light and so create the impression of a whitish bloom.

Meanwhile, 'white' objects can pick up numerous colourations and still appear acceptably white until compared with another 'white' that is differently complexioned. Indeed, a blue-based white may, to many people, look 'whiter' than a neutral white. Blue evokes coolness, and if the observer's personal criterion for a pure white is that it should have a cold feel, then this would explain the phenomenon. Although the purity of 'black' and 'white' could be defined purely in terms of their wavelength, it is the subjectivity of human vision that provides a chronic obstacle to full understanding of the psychological reality of black and white – especially when related to the worlds of partially or totally colour-blind people.

Someone who loses colour perception in a freak accident may be so traumatised by the event as to be unable to give any useful objective assessment of his or her new

Almost every professional photographer learns how to print in black and white. Their choices at this stage can be as important as the framing of the image itself, argues KRISTOFFER ALBRECHT

One reaction to all the colour and gloss in today's printed media is a return to expression in black and white. If one is striving towards a less technical impression, it is perhaps possible to learn something from a tradition of personal statements in the art of tones, from purest white to deepest black.

When a photograph is printed with ink on paper it is instantly translated into another medium. How and by whom this translation is carried out determines the whole being of the printed image.

The goal is generally to make the ink image resemble the original as much as possible, considering the technique, materials and financial resources at hand. The continuous tones of the original black and white photograph are faithfully simulated in the ink process. This way of working is natural and necessary when the satisfaction of the customer is guaranteed by results reached through standardisation of the process. The demands of economical realities are obvious. There is no room for much trial and error; unforeseen surprises are not welcome.

However, ever since the beginning of photography and photomechanical reproduction methods there has been a tradition to which flexibility seems to be more central than standardisation. If the ink-printed photograph is used as an independent means of expression – as art – the unanticipated surprises in the production process may be desirable because they enhance creativity.

For many photographers, producing ink-printed work has been central in their oeuvre. To these artists the printed image has been an art product equivalent to an original photograph. The photograph printed in ink is seen not merely as a picture of the artwork but as an entirely new thing, and, even in the ink-printed stage, explicitly as a work of art. In 1889, the Victorian photographic pioneer Peter Henry Emerson exclaimed: "if the photo-etching process [ie heliogravure] would become a lost art, we, for our part, would never take another photograph."

Within photographic art-printing the implementation of the artist's vision throughout the process becomes important. Without personal involvement artistic authenticity will be less likely to be found in the printed product. The artist should be in control of the entire production, possibly relying on the help of specialists in the printing trade. It is vital that the artist has a thorough knowledge of the proceedings and that

be or she understands the relations of the actions within the process. Due to the wide range of know-how that this requires, as well as to a traditional rivalry between trades, the mastering of every step in the process by one person is rare.

The American photographer and master-printer Richard Benson claims that issues within the area of tonal reproduction and printing can be meaningfully understood only by those who print themselves. He also points out that proper creation of the highest levels of tonal work in ink depend on flexibility throughout the stages.

Today's materials and techniques yield splendid results. Papers and inks are of extremely high quality and the presses are bigger and faster than ever before. Digital management systems make several previous intermediary steps superfluous. The products turned out by modern units are flashy, elegant and technically flawless. Nevertheless, they are often unoriginal, impersonal and cold.

Originality is reached by another kind of approach. The printed image can be given real features of individuality or of an attitude through a personal commitment to the production process.

KRISTOFFER ALBRECHT is a widely exhibited photographer and a Doctor of Arts from the University of Art and Design in Helsinki. He is the author of _Creative reproduction_, a practical study on inkprinted photographs, their history of production and aesthetic identity.

achromatic condition. The dramatic nature of abrupt disability places the focus on the shock of change rather than its resulting characteristics.

The loss of colour

In his essay _The Island of the Colour-Blind_, neurologist Oliver Sacks mentions the case history of an artist, Jonathan I, who, following a car accident, lost the ability to see colour or even to imagine or remember it. Nonetheless, he became haunted by a sense of deprivation, complaining that his world now seemed etiolated and somehow strangely depleted. In contrast, the person born with achromatopsia (total congenital colour-blindness) knows only his or her own greyscale reality, and, despite being obviously disadvantaged in a contemporary society that deploys colour-coded information so voluptuously, can have no idea what colour actually is and so does not miss it per se.

Also subjective – if easier to measure objectively – are the many variants of colour-blindness that exist between colour-normal vision and achromatopsia. Conventional colour-blindness tests can at least isolate and identify those colours that are being confused with one another. They also offer a clue as to why colour-blind personnel were sometimes used as camouflage spotters during World War II: undistracted by colour they were better than people with colour-normal vision at spotting the telltale shifts in surface and texture that betrayed the camouflaged installation.

Even in the colour-normal world (as we perceive it – different creatures have varying sensitivities to colour), this distracting nature of hues may be more potent than we sometimes think. When Peter Bogdanovich was interviewing Orson Welles about his career, he identified Welles' portrayal of Harry Lime in the 1949 movie _The Third Man_ as his most memorable performance. Welles replied that it was easy to give a memorable performance "because the film was in black and white". Bogdanovich, puzzled by the nonsequitur, asked him what he meant. "Name me a great performance in colour" was Welles' challenging reply. Thinking about it Bogdanovich was ruefully forced to admit that there was a grain of truth in the assertion. "In fact it is kind of hard to think of a great performance in colour," he concluded. Why should this be? Perhaps it's because black and white reduces everything, including the human face, to the bare essential information. We don't get distracted by how blue those blue eyes are...

One of the reasons it has been so hard to make a coherent assessment of how the achromatope might see the world is inherent in the nature of the condition itself. In the first place the number of sufferers is most great – perhaps one in 40,000 worldwide. In the second place the disease is typically accompanied by oversensitivity to light and poor overall visual acuity. As a result many achromatopes have in the past often been misdiagnosed and left to cope with a disability that prevented them from realising their full potential or in some cases even acquiring a basic education. It was not until one of their number overcame the considerable obstacles of his condition to become a distinguished physiologist and psycho-physicist at the University of Oslo that personal experience and scholarly converged to give the world – and fellow sufferers – new insights.

A different world view

Knut Nordby's account of his infancy and childhood as a sufferer from achromatopsia

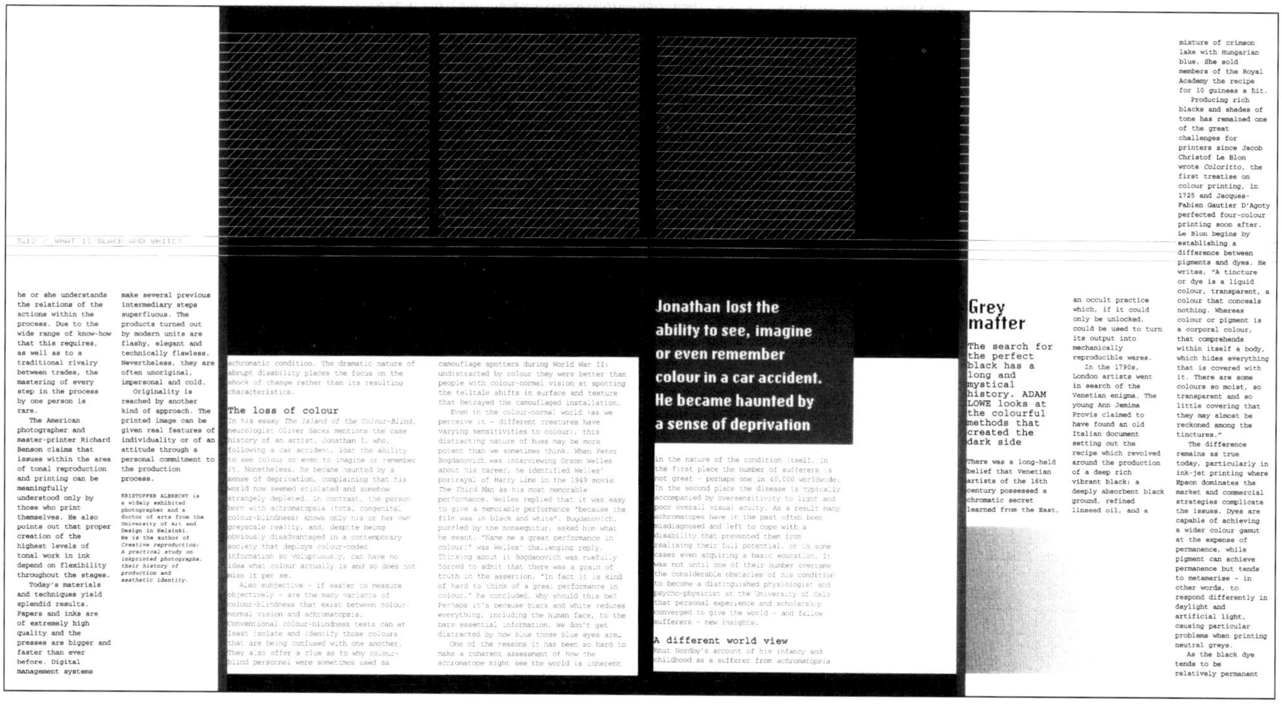

Jonathan lost the ability to see, imagine or even remember colour in a car accident. He became haunted by a sense of deprivation

Grey matter

The search for the perfect black has a long and mystical history. ADAM LOWE looks at the colourful methods that created the dark side

There was a long-held belief that Venetian artists of the 16th century possessed a chromatic secret learned from the East. an occult practice which, if it could only be unlocked, could be used to turn its output into mechanically reproducible wares.

In the 1790s, London artists went in search of the Venetian enigma. The young Ann Jemima Provis claimed to have found an old Italian document setting out the recipe which revolved around the production of a deep rich vibrant black: a deeply absorbent black ground, refined linseed oil, and a mixture of crimson lake with Hungarian blue. She sold members of the Royal Academy the recipe for 10 guineas a hit.

Producing rich blacks and shades of tone has remained one of the great challenges for printers since Jacob Christof Le Blon wrote _Coloritto_, the first treatise on colour printing, in 1725 and Jacques-Fabien Gautier D'Agoty perfected four-colour printing soon after. Le Blon begins by establishing a difference between pigments and dyes. He writes, "A tincture or dye is a liquid colour, transparent, a colour that conceals nothing. Whereas colour or pigment is a corporal colour, that comprehends within itself a body, which hides everything that is covered with it. There are some colours so moist, so transparent and so little covering that they may almost be reckoned among the tinctures."

The difference remains as true today, particularly in ink-jet printing where Epson dominates the market and commercial strategies complicate the issues. Dyes are capable of achieving a wider colour gamut at the expense of permanence, while pigment can achieve permanence but tends to metamerise – in other words, to respond differently in daylight and artificial light, causing particular problems when printing neutral greys.

As the black dye tends to be relatively permanent

Contained within a "belly band," each generously proportioned issue of _M-Real_ magazine engages readers with a different subject matter. Issue 5 goes back to basics and focuses on black and white. What better way to do this than by embracing the taxonomy of the typewriter and the computer? Text literally appears as it would within the monitor of a Mac or PC, while changes of scale and styles of letterforms create added drama, variety, texture, and tone. Stimulating use of space and grid is made throughout these exciting information-filled pages, incorporating areas of not only white, but also black background.

DESIGN FIRM **JOHN BROWN CITRUS PUBLISHING** ● CREATIVE DIRECTION **JEREMY LESLIE** ● CLIENT **M-REAL MAGAZINE** ● PROJECT NAME **M-REAL**

DESIGN FIRM **MIRKO ILIC** ● ART
DIRECTION **MIRKO ILIC** ● DESIGN
MIRKO ILIC, HEATH HINEGARDNER ●
COPY **LAETITIA WOLFF** ● CLIENT
FUTUREFLAIR ● PROJECT NAME
MASSIN POSTER

This poster announces and promotes a lecture and exhibition by French graphic designer Massin, whose most famous book design, we are told, is for *The Bald Soprano* by Ionesco. "THE POSTER REPRODUCES EVERY SPREAD OF THAT BOOK ON THE FRONT," says Mirko Ilic, "AND INCLUDES A DIAGRAM OF HOW TO CUT OUT AND ASSEMBLE YOUR OWN TINY VERSION ON THE REVERSE." In order to encompass all the text and imagery without stacking it in a classical horizontal layout, Mirko has coiled the spreads in a maze configuration that leads to the center and the title "Massin." The concept creates an extremely challenging layout that not only has to work two dimensionally, but also as a miniature book.

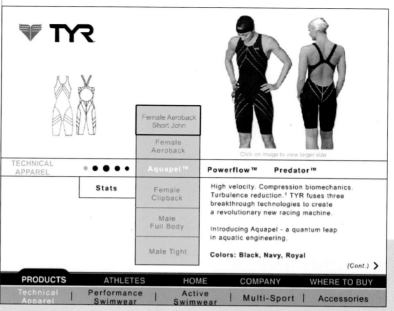

This online catalog for TYR Sport produced by [i]e design needed to accommodate lots of product shots and considerable amounts of information. Therefore, Marcie Carson and Cya Nelson derived a "disappearing collage" of imagery, which upon "rollover" vanishes to reveal a single large image. More detailed product information is presented within text- and diagram-rich pages. Readers are encouraged to stay with copy that often flows onto second screens. Space is obviously at a premium, "SO WE HAVE CONSTRUCTED A GRID, THAT HAS HELPED TO ORGANIZE INFORMATION AND HAS BECOME CONSISTENT THROUGHOUT, SO THAT USERS CAN EASILY ACCESS EACH SECTION AT ALL TIMES," says Alli Neiman.

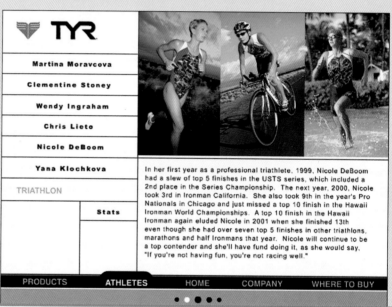

DESIGN FIRM [I]E DESIGN ● ART
DIRECTION MARCIE CARSON ●
DESIGN CYA NELSON ● CLIENT TYR
SPORT ● PROJECT NAME TYR SPORT
WEB SITE, WWW.TYR.COM

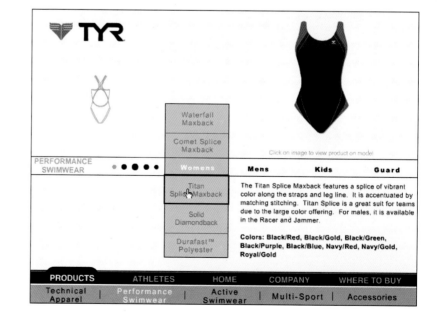

DESIGN FIRM **EXQUISITE CORPORATION** ● DESIGN **RILEY JOHN-DONNELL** ● COPY **JEREMY LIN** ● CLIENT: *SURFACE* MAGAZINE ● PROJECT NAME *SURFACE*

Energetic combinations of circles, angles, shaped picture boxes, and varying levels of type create three quite different and yet cohesive pages in this issue of *Surface* magazine.

Each covers a separate topic and, therefore, includes very disparate photographs and kinds of editorial, but the reader has no doubt that they all belong to the same section. Consistent typographic hierarchies, together with overt and covert replications of assorted circles and hexagons, maintain their identity and retain the readers' attention despite the many obligatory advertisements in between.

DESIGN FIRM **BAUMANN & BAUMANN**
● COPY **BAUMANN & BAUMANN** ●
ILLUSTRATION **BAUMANN & BAUMANN**
● PHOTOGRAPHY **BAUMANN &**
BAUMANN ● CLIENT **SELF-PROMOTION**
● PROJECT NAME *ROOM TO MOVE*

Most of the pages in *Room to Move*, as the title suggests, are extravagant explorations of generous space and "graphic fun." These two spreads, however, reverse the emphasis and reflect the mass of information, names, and histories that appeared in the exhibition Baumann & Baumann designed for the Hohenasperg prison in Germany. The contextual details are in German and English, and the complex interplay of purple and white type communicates a great deal of information about the prison, as well as being aesthetically enjoyable. By changing the scales, weights, and colors of the type, words and text can overlap and interweave, yet still retain legibility.

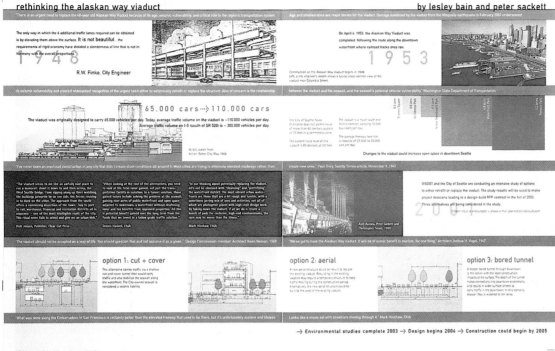

rethinking the alaskan way viaduct   by lesley bain and peter sackett

1948

The only way in which the 6 additional traffic lanes required can be obtained is by elevating them above the surface. It is not beautiful...the requirements of rigid economy have dictated a slenderness of line that is not in harmony with the overall proportions.

R.W. Finke, City Engineer

1953

On April 4, 1953, the Alaskan Way Viaduct was completed, following the route along the downtown waterfront where railroad tracks once ran.

65,000 cars → 110,000 cars

The viaduct was originally designed to carry 65,000 vehicles per day. Today, average traffic volume on the viaduct is ~110,000 vehicles per day. Average traffic volume on I-5 (south of SR 520) is ~300,000 vehicles per day.

Changes to the viaduct could increase open space in downtown Seattle

WSDOT and the City of Seattle are conducting an intensive study of options to either retrofit or replace the viaduct. The study results will be used to make project decisions leading to a design-build RFP contract in the fall of 2003. Three alternatives are being considered in the study.

option 1: cut + cover

option 2: aerial

option 3: bored tunnel

→ Environmental studies complete 2003 → Design begins 2004 → Construction could begin by 2005

---

review

architectural banquet fare
2001 AIBC/ lieutenant-governor design awards disappoint

"IT QUICKLY BECAME EVIDENT," says Karen Cheng of the University of Washington, **"THAT ANY DESIGN FOR ARCADE HAD TO ACCOMMODATE A HIGH DENSITY OF INFORMATION."** To take up as little space as possible, the text is in Rotis (a condensed typeface) in a small point size with fairly close leading. The column width is quite wide, and justified typesetting with hyphenations enables a maximum word count per line. This leaves the greatest amount of space possible for clear large-scale photographs, and a dynamic headline using type as image, that overlaps the copy and plays a significant part in integrating the spread as a whole.

Two-color print has the ability to unite pages in a publication, despite differing treatments. Cheng's spread on rethinking the Alaskan way viaduct, although using the same typeface, is a contrasting interplay of changing column widths, red and black type, and powerful horizontal bands that take the reader from left to right without recognition of a spinal division.

DESIGN FIRM **UNIVERSITY OF WASHINGTON** ● DESIGN **KAREN CHENG** ● CLIENT *ARCADE* MAGAZINE ● PROJECT NAME *ARCADE*

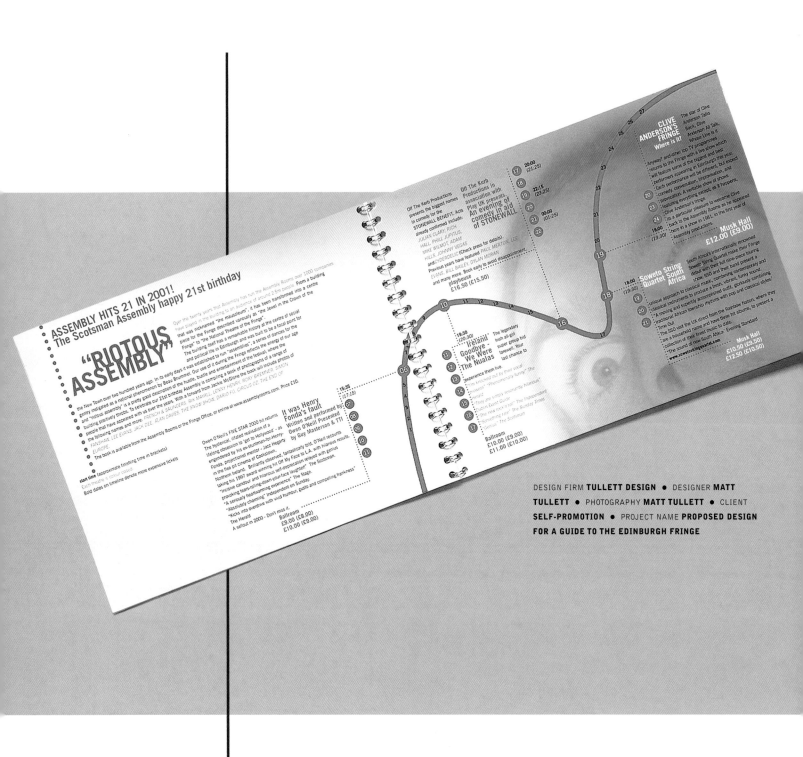

DESIGN FIRM **TULLETT DESIGN** ● DESIGNER **MATT TULLETT** ● PHOTOGRAPHY **MATT TULLETT** ● CLIENT **SELF-PROMOTION** ● PROJECT NAME **PROPOSED DESIGN FOR A GUIDE TO THE EDINBURGH FRINGE**

column of many orders

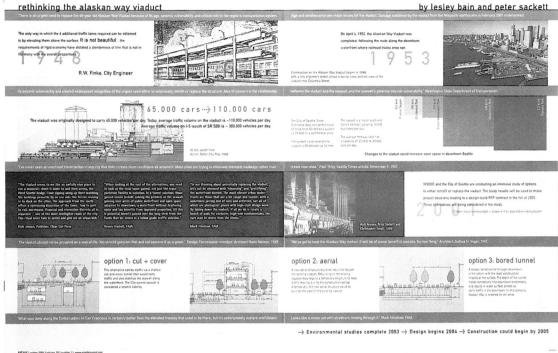

rethinking the alaskan way viaduct   by lesley bain and peter sackett

review

"IT QUICKLY BECAME EVIDENT," says Karen Cheng of the University of Washington, **"THAT ANY DESIGN FOR ARCADE HAD TO ACCOMMODATE A HIGH DENSITY OF INFORMATION."** To take up as little space as possible, the text is in Rotis (a condensed typeface) in a small point size with fairly close leading. The column width is quite wide, and justified typesetting with hyphenations enables a maximum word count per line. This leaves the greatest amount of space possible for clear large-scale photographs, and a dynamic headline using type as image, that overlaps the copy and plays a significant part in integrating the spread as a whole.

Two-color print has the ability to unite pages in a publication, despite differing treatments. Cheng's spread on rethinking the Alaskan way viaduct, although using the same typeface, is a contrasting interplay of changing column widths, red and black type, and powerful horizontal bands that take the reader from left to right without recognition of a spinal division.

DESIGN FIRM **UNIVERSITY OF WASHINGTON** • DESIGN **KAREN CHENG** • CLIENT *ARCADE* MAGAZINE • PROJECT NAME *ARCADE*

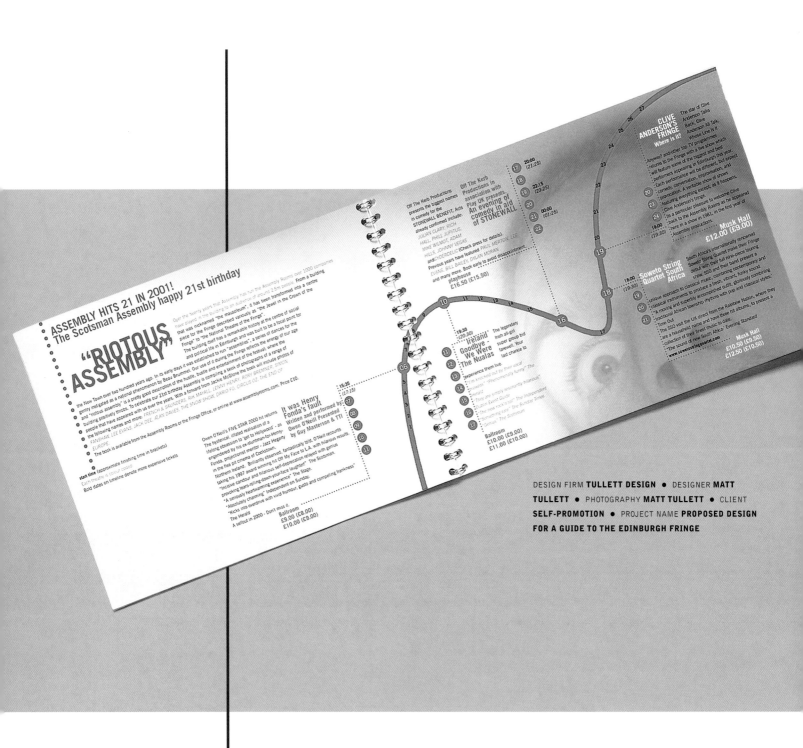

DESIGN FIRM **TULLETT DESIGN** ● DESIGNER **MATT TULLETT** ● PHOTOGRAPHY **MATT TULLETT** ● CLIENT **SELF-PROMOTION** ● PROJECT NAME **PROPOSED DESIGN FOR A GUIDE TO THE EDINBURGH FRINGE**

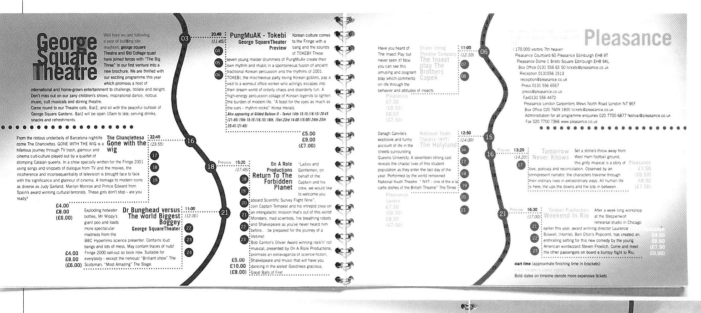

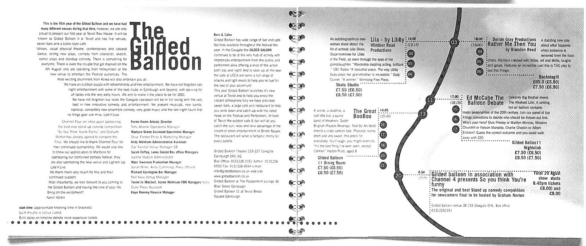

Within this proposed design for a guide to the "Edinburgh fringe," newly graduated designer Matt Tullett managed to beautifully and successfully accommodate a huge amount of information within limited space. Tullett has originated a flexible calendar that snakes across many pages, providing interesting divisions of space. "THIS DATE SYSTEM ALLOWS FOR VARIED QUANTITIES OF INFORMATION TO BE GROUPED IN INTERESTING AND DIVERSE WAYS," says Tullett, "HELPING TO MAKE BEST USE OF THE BROCHURE'S SMALL FORMAT" (6.4" × 8.25", 16 cm × 21 cm). The details for each individual event are linked to Tullett's calendar by bold dotted lines that fulfill the role of defining an area of individual space for each production.

DESIGN FIRM **SK VISUAL** ● ART
DIRECTION **SPENCER LUM, KATYA
LYUMKIS** ● DESIGN **KATYA LYUMKIS**
● CLIENT **SABBIA MARE** ● PROJECT
NAME **SABBIA MARE WEB SITE,**
WWW.SABBIAMARE.COM

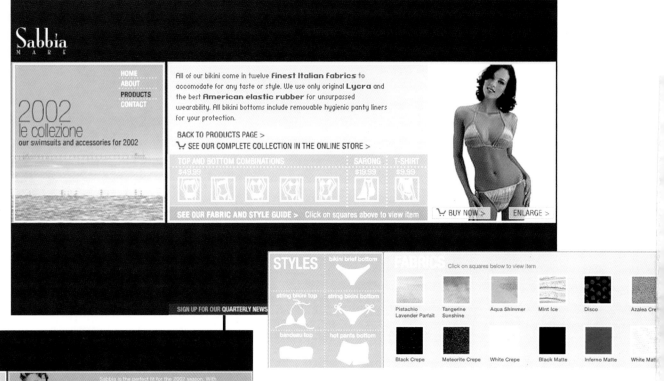

Promising us the "perfect bikini," Sabbia Mare is a new brand that has set out to create a distinctive online presence. "WE USED A COMBINATION OF POP-UP WINDOWS AND FLASH LOADING SEQUENCES TO CLARIFY THE INFORMATION AND ENABLE CERTAIN ITEMS TO BE ACCESSED FROM MULTIPLE PAGES," says Katya Lyumkis of SK Visual. The fabric swatch matrix is compact, while maintaining its relevancy to most of the site. Dividing the complex data into individual pop-up windows enables the viewer to access certain items from a number of pages without losing sight of primary information.

Victims of domestic violence invariably are too scared or ashamed to tell anyone about their problems. We have designed a series of miniature leaflets that fold to the size of a credit card and can be hidden in a purse or wallet. They contain a lot of information and because they are for a multicultural community, they are produced in English and three Asian languages. In many respects, these leaflets are predominantly functional, so the layout needs to group numbers, addresses, and advice in easily understood ways. However, we wanted to make them as visually appealing as possible to encourage people to pick up, and also to appear bright and positive about very sad circumstances. Despite the limited space, we achieved hierarchy through changes in size, weight, and color, and movement through asymmetric arrangements.

DESIGN FIRM **BRIGHT PINK** ● DESIGN **JESSICA GLASER, CAROLYN KNIGHT** ● CLIENT **WOLVERHAMPTON DOMESTIC VIOLENCE FORUM** ● PROJECT NAME **SURVIVAL CARDS**

wheel
of fortune

FORGET TRADITIONAL END-OF-THE-PIER DISTRACTIONS: THE MODERN AMUSEMENT RIDE IS A MULTI-MILLION DOLLAR HI-TECH EXPERIMENT, DEVOTED TO TAKING YOU HIGHER, FURTHER AND FASTER THAN EVER BEFORE. *HOT AIR* INVESTIGATES THE SCIENCE OF THEME PARKS

TEXT **DAVID BAKER**

Eddie Newquist knows a lot about theme parks. As president of film and production at BBH, a firm of park and exhibit designers based in San Antonio, Texas, it's his job to be up to speed on every single innovation in the sector. He has worked with some of the world's biggest entertainment "franchises", from *Terminator* to *Jurassic Park*; he has produced films designed to be seen in three dimensions or through 360 degrees; he is, in the words of his company's corporate website, "an industry innovator, holding patents for developing advanced motion picture/show systems and for designing high-capacity entertainment experiences". He is, in short, devoted to pushing theme parks to ever more ambitious extremes – to making their attractions ever faster, bigger, better and more sophisticated. But even he knows that, however much technology he may have to show off with, there is one line that should never be crossed. "Some of the new rides on show at the IAAPA [the industry's trade body, the International Association of Amusement Parks and Attractions] convention last year were not successful," he recalls. "They just made people sick. If someone comes off a ride and they're feeling sick then they are not going to want to buy things. And you certainly don't want that."

You certainly don't: organised fun is big business and last year, theme parks in the US took $9.6bn from 317m happy punters. In the EU, theme park turnover topped $1.5m and Alton Towers, the UK's most popular theme park, welcomed 2.45m people through its gates. Tokyo Disneyland, the best attended theme park in the world, entertained an even more impressive 16m visitors. But what exactly is it that draws people to shoot down an artificial river while being splashed by fake white water, queue for more than an hour to be dropped 200ft in a cage, or clamber into crude body harnesses to be hurled towards rocks at 90mph?

"Theme parks offer two distinct attractions," explains Glenn Wilson, a psychologist at the Institute of Psychiatry in London, who has made a speciality of researching the industry. "Firstly, they provide a fantasy world, an opportunity for children to lose themselves and for adults to return to childhood; and secondly they give you the chance to rise to the challenge presented by the thrill rides."

The idea of a "fantasy world" was the first defining feature of the theme park. Back in the early 50s, Walt Disney's brief to the designers who were to build Disneyland in California was simple: "I just want it to look like nothing else in the world. And it should be surrounded by a train." Disneyland's Main Street, two rows of impossibly pristine Victorian shops, businesses, bars and restaurants (some fake, some real) is built on a ¾ scale. "This cost more," said Disney, "but it has turned the street into a toy and the imagination can play more freely with a toy."

If that toytown aesthetic was the first distinct feature of the theme park, though, these days the most important ingredients are not the theatrical looks, but the thrill rides – the roller-coasters, haunted houses and spinning wheels with names like XLR-8, Spider and Vortex, that make the adrenalin run through the body and pull punters through the gates. "It's very easy to terrify a person," says John Wardley, an independent ride designer for the Tussaud's Group and the man behind such cutting-edge attractions as Nemesis and Oblivion, both at Alton Towers, "but that isn't always entertainment. I am essentially an entertainer. When you design a ride you have the whole spectrum of emotions to play with – you can make them surprised, amazed, baffled, intrigued, scared – and you do that by giving the ride a story, a rhythm. With a white-knuckle ride, the story might be quite simple, but it is still there: you want to challenge them before they get on – dare you do it? You want to give them an intense and thrilling experience in the middle; and you want them to have a feeling of exhilaration at the end that they have got the better of it and have survived." The process of putting this ideal into practice is where the science of theme parks really comes to the fore.

THEME PARK RIDES CAN BE DIVIDED INTO THREE BROAD GROUPS: dark rides, where participants are transported through the interior of a warehouse-like structure and are exposed to projections, animatronics, special effects and, hopefully, adrenalin; iron rides, the free-standing spinning wheels or rocking boats that are a feature of every fair; and roller coasters – the T-Rexes of the theme park world.

When it comes to storytelling, the dark rides understandably rule the roost. Thanks to advanced audio-visuals and super-detailed 70mm film, parabolic screens as high as houses and multi-channel sound, you can transport the riders to outer space or the centre of the Earth at the flick of a switch. Your scene can be peopled with animatronics – realistic robots that are programmed to speak and move when triggered by a car's approach – although some park owners prefer actors because they're cheaper. Add special effects, such as fog or fire, to help the audience forget where they are, so that, for five minutes or so, they fly like Superman, or at least get to think they're Indiana Jones.

"Dark rides give you an incredible opportunity to make people feel like heroes," says dark ride scriptwriter Tim Beedle, "because no other medium lets you have the audience playing such an active role." Beedle works for JPI Design in Ontario, California, a park and ride design company that has just begun work on Adventure World, a $40m theme park just outside of Jeddah, Saudi Arabia. "Writing for dark rides is like writing for theatre or the movies. You map things out scene by scene but the extra dimension is that the audience can be characters in the story too. They are no longer just passive viewers."

Adventure World is a conversion project – there is a small theme park already on the site which JPI is to expand and improve upon. There is an existing dark ride, a kind of runaway-train-in-a-mine attraction, and one of JPI's briefs is to recast it as something more interesting.

"What we are doing," says Beedle, "is taking that attraction and changing the story. We have a specific layout to the ride that can't change – except that we can alter the speed of the train. We came up with a King Solomon's Mines/Indiana Jones theme, which is fairly new to Middle Eastern audiences. The mine will become an archeological dig where an ancient burial chamber has just been uncovered. The audience becomes visiting scientists invited to view the discovery." This is the backstory – the explanation of what has happened and why

Investigating the science of theme parks designed to take us, higher, faster, and further than before, "Wheel of Fortune" successfully integrates unusual photography with a considerable volume of text. Words extend across pale slabs of background image while located firmly within a grid structure. Images overlap and are juxtaposed with a number of unusual crops, creating pleasing and unpredictable groupings. Information generally fills the pages, with the only relief being established by vast expanses of blue sky that give the sea of text some life and make it seem more manageable.

THE QUEUE IS DESIGNED SO THAT THE TRACK GOES RIGHT OVER PEOPLE'S HEADS. THEY CAN HEAR THE SCREAMS AS THE CARS GO PAST. THIS SENDS THEIR ANTICIPATION THROUGH THE ROOF UNTIL THEY ARE GOING CRAZY

DESIGN FIRM **JOHN BROWN CITRUS PUBLISHING** ● ART DIRECTION **WARREN JACKSON** ● COPY **DAVID BAKER** ● ILLUSTRATION **CHRIS WINN** ● CLIENT **VIRGIN ATLANTIC** ● PROJECT NAME *HOT AIR*, "WHEEL OF FORTUNE"

DESIGN FIRM **JOHN BROWN CITRUS PUBLISHING** ● ART DIRECTION **SIMON ROBINSON** ● DESIGN **CLARE WATTERS** ● COPY **JO SPELLING** ● CLIENT *O* **MAGAZINE** ● PROJECT NAME **INNOVATION AND TRAVEL PAGES**

The two pages in this spread are on different topics, and the challenge for any designer in these circumstances is to create clear differentiation, while maintaining cohesion. The illustration with the blue background plays a key role in separating the articles, but it also is significant in setting up visual links with the other page, as blues and oranges are recognized in all type and imagery. The margins and narrow column widths are the same on both pages, and more subtly, but not to be overlooked, the configuration of the squared-up images on the left replicates the general shape and proportions formed by the British Isles.

DESIGN FIRM **SCORSONE/DRUEDING** ●
ART DIRECTION **JOE SCORSONE, ALICE
DRUEDING** ● COPY **JOE SCORSONE,
ALICE DRUEDING** ● ILLUSTRATION **JOE
SCORSONE, ALICE DRUEDING** ●
CLIENT **SELF-PROMOTION** ● PROJECT
NAME **CONFESS**

As the latest in a wide-ranging series of Scorsone/Drueding self-promotional posters, this one focuses on the act of confession. From a distance, the viewer gets the impression that the confessor is communicating with a "higher authority," with no other information given. However, on closer examination it is apparent that the many, many sins of the confessor fill every available space, even flowing around the illustrations and covering the most awkward areas. The poster includes a seemingly endless list of misdemeanors to which a person can confess and has presented them in a handwritten, personal way in order to appear more visually interesting and appropriate.

DESIGN FIRM **FELTON COMMUNICATIONS** ●
DESIGNER **BRION FURNELL** ● COPY
RICHARD SCHOLEY ● CLIENT **TERRANCE**
HIGGINS TRUST ● PROJECT NAME **ISSUE 13**

Issue 13 is an eight-page accordion-fold information brochure for the Terrance Higgins Trust.

Covering the gay men's HIV-prevention initiative, the layouts are filled with detailed advice and statistical information. "Vital Statistics" presents a considerable amount of information in a helpful and accessible way, with sectioned copy appearing in individual colored boxes. This has the effect of encouraging the viewer to read random selections in bite-size chunks, so even if eventually the entire text is covered, it does not feel too daunting.

The directory of *American Photography* 17 contains even more information than typically found in index sections, featuring full-color photographs, address details, publishing information, and descriptions. Far from being a dull and rather practical necessity, it creates a lively composition using alternatives of scale, color, and type to visually code the different hierarchies, and a green background tint to helpfully differentiate the left column from the right. As the main body of the book had to present one image per page in a fairly static manner, the changing rhythms of the index spreads add welcome contrast and character.

DESIGN FIRM **344 DESIGN** ● DESIGN **STEFAN G. BUCHER** ● CLIENT **AMILUS, INC.** ● PROJECT NAME ***AMERICAN PHOTOGRAPHY* 17**

one

swallow

does not

make a

spring

In the bird-watching haven of England's northwest coast, there is to be a found a newly opened typographic path.

This narrow creation runs for 98.5 feet (300 m) and contains innumerable examples of poems, song lyrics, and traditional sayings that focus on the topic of birds. Flock of Words starts at the very beginning with Genesis and stretches through a variety of informative, educational, and entertaining pieces, ranging from Shakespeare to Spike Milligan.

"WE HAD A LOT OF INFORMATION TO ACCOMMODATE AND A VERY NARROW FORMAT TO FILL," says Andy Altmann of Why Not Associates. "IN ADDITION TO THIS, THE FOOTPATH IS ACCESSED AT MANY POINTS AND FROM MANY DIFFERENT ANGLES, REQUIRING THE DESIGN TO FUNCTION ON A DECORATIVE LEVEL AS WELL AS BEING A SOURCE OF INFORMATION."

In addition to featuring sections of the tremendously detailed design sheets for this piece, a selection of fascinating cameos show the construction process. This seldom seen skill of the on-site assembly of architectural typography reveals the considerable challenge of accommodating type within such a long, narrow format.

DESIGN FIRM **WHY NOT ASSOCIATES**
● DESIGNERS **WHY NOT ASSOCIATES**
● PHOTOGRAPHY **PHOTODISC, ROCCO REDONDO** ● CLIENT **LANCASTER CITY COUNCIL** ● PROJECT NAME **FLOCK OF WORDS**

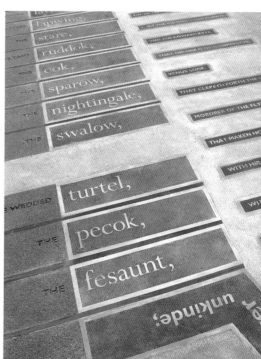

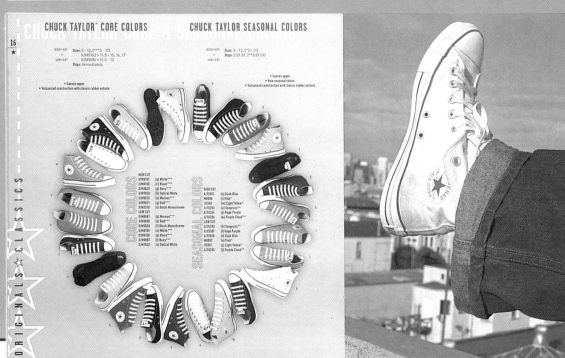

DESIGN FIRM **BLACKCOFFEE** ● ART
DIRECTION **MARK GALLAGHER** ●
DESIGN **LAURA SAVARD** ●
PHOTOGRAPHY **DAVID BRADLEY**
PHOTOGRAPHY ● CLIENT **CONVERSE**
● PROJECT NAME **CONVERSE CATALOG**

**"CONVERSE'S CHALLENGE WAS TO DEVELOP A CATALOG
WHERE THE PRODUCT WOULD 'JUMP OFF
THE PAGE,'"** says Laura Savard, and with such a large
range of shoes this is no small task. Blackcoffee has used
photography mainly to inform the reader, cleverly
displaying cut-out group shots of every design and color of
sneaker available alongside contrasting large-scale,
squared-up lifestyle images. "A SILVER-TINTED
VARNISH FLOODS THE NEGATIVE SPACE, FORCING
THE IMAGES TO POP FORWARD AND DEMAND
ATTENTION," Savard adds.

DIRECTORY

344 DESIGN LLC
101 N. Grand Avenue Suite 7
Pasadena CA 91103 USA
T: 626 796 5148

AIGA BOSTON CHAPTER
One Design Center Place
Boston MA 02210 USA
T: 617 330 1007 F: 617 330 1004

APPETITE ENGINEERS
218 Noe Street
San Francisco CA 94114 USA
T: 415 252 8122

BAUMANN & BAUMANN
Taubentalstrasse 4/1
73525 Schwäbisch Gmünd
Germany
T: 7171 927990 F: 7171 927999

BBC DESIGN BRISTOL
Whiteladies Road
Bristol BS8 2LR UK
T: 0117 974 2175

BECK GRAPHIC DESIGN
Messinastrasse 13
FI-9494 Triesen Leichtenstein
Germany
T: 041 753 900930
F: 041 753 900931

BELYEA
1809 Seventh Avenue Suite 1250
Seattle WA 98101 USA
T: 206 682 4895 F: 206 623 8912

BLACKCOFFEE
840 Summer Street
Boston MA 02127 USA
T: 617 268 1116

BRIGHT PINK
Lapley Studio
Lapley
Stafford ST19 9JS UK
T: 01785 841601 F: 01785 841401

BÜRO FÜR GESTALTUNG
Domstrasse 81
Offenbach D-63067 Germany
T: 069 881424 F: 069 881423

CPD DESIGN
333 Flinders Lane
Second Floor
Melbourne Victoria 3000 Australia
T: 613 9620 5911

DIGITAL VISION LTD.
India House
45 Curlew Street
London SE1 2ND UK
T: 0207 378 5500

DWELL
99 Osgood Place
San Francisco CA 94133 USA
T: 415 743 9990 F: 415 743 9978

EXUISITE CORPORATION
7 Isadora Duncan Lane
San Francisco CA 94102 USA
T: 415 929 5112 F: 415 929 5103

FELTON COMMUNICATION
2 Bleeding Heart Yard
Farringdon London EC1N 8SJ UK
T: 0207 405 0900

FISHTEN
1219 14th Avenue SW
Calgary AL T3C 0W1 Canada
T: 403 228 7959

GEE + CHUNG DESIGN
38 Bryant Street
Suite 100
San Francisco CA 94105 USA
T: 415 543 1192 F: 415 543 6088

GREENFIELD/BELSER LTD.
1818N Street
Washington DC 20036 USA
T: 202 775 0333 F: 202 775 0402

GROUP BARONET
2200 N Lamar #201
Dallas TX 7520 USA
T: 214 954 0316

HAT-TRICK DESIGN
3 Morocco Street
London SE1 3HB UK
T: 0207 403 7875

HAYMARKET PUBLISHING
60 Waldegrave Road
Teddington
Middlesex TW11 8LG UK
T: 0208 267 5104

HÉPA! DESIGNS
402-27 Alexander Street
Vancouver BC V6A 1B2 Canada
T: 604 608 2424

HOLLER
26 Shacklewell Lane
London E8 2EZ UK
T: 0207 6900416

IDAHO
Greenheys Business Center
10 Pencroft Way
Manchester M15 6JT UK
T: 0161 232 1777

IDENTIKAL
Studio 5
The Oasis Building
Empire Square
London N7 6JN UK
T: 0207 263 2129
F: 0207 272 1521

THE INDEPENDENT NEWSPAPER
191 Marsh Wall
London E2 9BD UK
T: 0207 005 2628

INFOGRAPHICS DESIGN
P.O. Box 66
Newtown NSW Australia
T: 612 9519 4225

INTERBRAND
130 Fifth Avenue
New York NY 10011 USA
T: 212 798 7500 F: 212 798 7501

I[E] DESIGN
1600 Rosecrans Avenue #6B/2C
Manhattan Beach CA 90266 USA
T: 310 727 3515

JOHN BROWN CITRUS PUBLISHING
136-142 Bramley Road
London W10 6SR UK
T: 0207 565 3000

KARACTERS DESIGN GROUP
777 Hornby Street Stuite 1600
Vancouver BC V672T3 Canada
T: 604 640 4348

KATIE GARDNER DESIGN
57 Bromford Rise
Oaklands Road
Wolverhampton WV3 0ES UK

KROG
Krakovski Nasip 22
1000 Ljubljana Slovenia
T: 41 780 880

KYM ABRAMS DESIGN
213W Institute Place Suite 608
Chicago IL 60610 USA
T: 312 654 9664 F: 312 654 0665

LAUREY ROBIN BENNETT DESIGN
10584 Bradbury Road
Los Angeles CA 90046 USA
T: 310 837 2126

LOVE
72 Tib Street
Manchester M4 1LG UK
T: 0161 907 3154

MATT AND GEORGE
14 Greek Street
Soho London W10 4DW UK
T: 0207 434 7183

MEDIA CELL LTD.
10-16 Tiller Road
Docklands London E14 8PY UK
T: 0207 987 6166

METALLI LINDBERG
Viale Venezia
135 Conegliano
Treviso Italy
T: 0438 656611 F: 0438 656677

MIRKO ILIC CORP.
207E 32 Street
New York NY 10016 USA
T: 212 481 9737

MONSTER DESIGN
7826 Leary Way NE #200
Redmond WA 98052 USA
T: 425 823 7853 F: 425 576 8055

MOTOKO HADA
69-45 108th Street #9E
Forest Hills
New York NY 11375 USA
T: 718 268 2592

NIKLAUS TROXLER DESIGN
Postfach Willisau
CH-6130 Switzerland
T: 041 970 2731 F: 041 970 3231

ODED EZER DESIGN STUDIO
9/2 Bloch Street
Givat Ayim 53229 Israel
T: 3 672 5489

ORIGIN DESIGN
10 Cambridge Terrace
Wellington New Zealand
T: 04 801 6644

PAPRIKA
400 Laurier Ouest #610
Montreal Québec H2V 2K7 Canada
T: 514 276-6000 F: 514 276-6100

PHILIP FASS
1310 State Street
Cedar Falls IA 50613 4128 USA
T: 319 273 7278 F: 319 273 7333

PING PONG DESIGN
Rochussenstraat 400
Rotterdam 301526 Netherlands
T: 010 4365744

PISCATELLO DESIGN CENTRE
355 Seventh Avenue Suite 304
New York NY 10001 USA
T: 212 502 4734 F: 212 502 4735

PURDUE UNIVERSITY
1352 CA-1
West Lafayette IN 47907 USA
T: 765 494 3072 F: 765 496 1198

RECHORD
New Media Labs
Watford Road
Harrow HA1 3TP UK
T: 0208 357 7322

RED COMMUNICATIONS
155 Dalhousie Street #524
Toronto ON M5B 2P7 Canada
T: 416 831 0733

RIORDEN DESIGN GROUP INC.
131 George Street
Oakville ON L6J 3B9 Canada
T: 905 339 0750

RIPTIDE COMMUNICATIONS
38 West 38th Street Fifth Floor
New York NY 10018 USA
T: 212 840 0309

ROUNDEL
7 Rosehart Mews
Westbourne Grove
London W11 3TY UK
T: 0207 221 1951

SAGMEISTER INC.
222 West 14th Street
New York NY 10011 USA
T: 212 647 1789

SAYLES GRAPHIC DESIGN
3701 Beaver Avenue
Des Moines IA 50310 USA
T: 515 279 2922 F:515 279 0212

SCANDINAVIAN DESIGN GROUP
Pakhus 12
Dampfærgevej 8
Copenhagen OE DK2100 Denmark
F: 035 270102 T: 035 270151

SCORSONE/DRUEDING
2/2 Greenwood Avenue
Jenkintown PA 19046 USA
T: 215 572 0782

SILVIA VALLIM DESIGN
Avenue Princesa Isabel 323 Sl. 1107
Rio de Janeiro 22011 010 Brazil
T: 55 21 2295 1976

SK VISUAL
250 West 50th Street #10L
New York NY 10019 USA
T: 212 956 0077

SPLASH INTERACTIVE
99 Harbour Square Suite 2112
Toronto ON M5J 2H2 Canada
T: 416 928 0465 F: 416 922 1683

STUDIO VERTEX
505 14th Avenue E #301
Seattle WA 48112 USA
T: 206 849 3901

TEIKNA DESIGN INC.
192 Spadina Avenue Suite 407
Toronto ON 15T 2C2 Canada
T: 416 504 8668 F: 416 504 2626

TRICKETT AND WEBB
The Factory
84 Marchmont Street
London WC1N 1AG UK
T: 0207 388 5832

TULLETT DESIGN
20 Sherwood Road
Smethwick
West Midlands B67 5DE UK
T: 0121 420 1886

**UNIVERSITY OF WASHINGTON
SCHOOL OF ART**
Box 353440
Seattle WA 98195 USA
T: 206 685 2773 F: 206 685 1657

WAGNER DESIGN
455 E Eisenhower
Ann Arbor MI 48108 USA
T: 734 429 3440

WHY NOT ASSOCIATES
22C Shepherdess Walk
London N1 7LB UK
T: 0207 253 2244

WILSON HARVEY
Sir John Lyon House
High Timber Street
London E24V 3NX UK
T: 0207 4207700

Y+R 2.1
100 First Street
San Francisco CA 94105 USA
T: 415 882 0600 F: 415 882 0745

Z3
Loft 2
Broughton Works
27 George Street
Birmingham B3 1QG UK
T: 0121 233 2545
F: 0121 233 2544

Carolyn Knight and Jessica Glaser are partners at BRIGHT PINK COMMUNICATION DESIGN. Their clients come from areas including building and property, charities, textiles, horticulture, education, and health care. Bright Pink is a full-service firm specializing in copywriting and art direction for brochures, annual reports, visual identities, packaging, exhibitions, and Web sites.

As associate lecturers at the UNIVERSITY OF WOLVERHAMPTON'S SCHOOL OF ART AND DESIGN, Knight and Glaser deliver lectures and modules concerning the practical and theoretical aspects of typography, page layout, visual identity, and Web site design.